Pretensions of Objectivity

Pretensions of Objectivity

—— Toward a Criticism of Biblical Criticism ——

Jeffrey L. Morrow

☙PICKWICK *Publications* · Eugene, Oregon

PRETENSIONS OF OBJECTIVITY
Toward a Criticism of Biblical Criticism

Copyright © 2019 Jeffrey L. Morrow. All rights reserved. Except for brief quotations in critical publications or reviews, no part of this book may be reproduced in any manner without prior written permission from the publisher. Write: Permissions, Wipf and Stock Publishers, 199 W. 8th Ave., Suite 3, Eugene, OR 97401.

Pickwick Publications
An Imprint of Wipf and Stock Publishers
199 W. 8th Ave., Suite 3
Eugene, OR 97401

www.wipfandstock.com

PAPERBACK ISBN: 978-1-5326-5738-2
HARDCOVER ISBN: 978-1-5326-5739-9
EBOOK ISBN: 978-1-5326-5740-5

Cataloguing-in-Publication data:

Names: Morrow, Jeffrey Lawrence, 1978–, author.

Title: Pretensions of objectivity : toward a criticism of biblical criticism / by Jeffrey L. Morrow.

Description: Eugene, OR : Pickwick Publications, 2019 | Includes bibliographical references and index.

Identifiers: ISBN 978-1-5326-5738-2 (paperback) | ISBN 978-1-5326-5739-9 (hardcover) | ISBN 978-1-5326-5740-5 (ebook)

Subjects: LCSH: Bible—Criticism, interpretation, etc. | Criticism, interpretation, etc.

Classification: BS511.3 .M70 2019 (print) | BS511.3 .M70 (ebook)

Manufactured in the U.S.A.   03/07/19

This book is dedicated to my loving wife Maria, my best friend and travelling companion in this life on our pilgrimage to heaven.

Contents

Acknowledgments | ix

Introduction | 1

1 Back to the Source: Biblical Criticism in the Renaissance and Reformation | 10

2 Corrosive History: Pioneer Biblical Critics | 35

3 The Brave New World of Seventeenth-Century Biblical Interpretation | 55

4 A Genealogy of Catholic Notions of Inspiration | 75

5 Secularization and the Elusive Quest for Objective Biblical Interpretation | 92

Conclusion | 107

Bibliography | 109
Subject Index | 127
Author Index | 129

Acknowledgments

THIS PRESENT VOLUME BEGAN from research over a number of years that resulted in presentations, published journal articles, as well as a lengthy book review essay. The first and third chapters began as a book review essay of Scott Hahn and Benjamin Wiker's *Politicizing the Bible: The Roots of Historical Criticism and the Secularization of Scripture 1300–1700*. The earlier review that served as the basis for these two chapters was originally published as, "Averroism, Nominalism, and Mechanization: Hahn and Wiker's Unmasking of Historical Criticism's Political Agenda by Laying Bare its Philosophical Roots" in *Nova et Vetera*. These two chapters represent a greatly revised and modified version of that earlier essay, material from which is reused here with permission, for which I thank *Nova et Vetera*.

The second chapter began as research for a project done at the invitation of Matthew Levering for a presentation on the history of biblical interpretation leading up to the Second Vatican Council. I was unable to present the paper due to the birth of my son Patrick, but I eventually completed the project. The second half of that paper—which focuses upon Fr. Richard Simon and St. Thomas More—was published in *New Blackfriars*, then expanded, revised, and included in my book, *Theology, Politics, and Exegesis: Essays on the History of Modern Biblical Criticism*. The first half of that paper, however, was published as, "The Acid of History: La Peyrère, Hobbes, Spinoza, and the Separation of Faith and Reason in Modern Biblical Studies" in *Heythrop Journal*. I thank *Heythrop Journal* for their permission to use the piece, now thoroughly revised and modified, as the basis for this second chapter.

The fourth chapter began as research I conducted for a presentation to doctoral students and Franciscan Friars of the Renewal for the Letter & Spirit Summer Institute, which Scott Hahn invited me to present in 2008. The presentation was entitled, "Modern Biblical Interpretation and the Sacramental Hermeneutic." I thank Scott Hahn and Michael Hahn for their helpful comments on that presentation, as well as all of the participants who helped me think through that material and encouraged me to pursue the subject matter further. My continued research on the topic resulted in the article, "The Modernist Crisis and the Shifting of Catholic Views on Biblical Inspiration," in *Letter & Spirit*. I later revised and significantly modified that work, reusing it here, in chapter four, with permission, for which I thank *Letter & Spirit*.

The fifth and final chapter began as research which I presented in my conference presentation, "The Theological Politics of the Quest for Objectivity: The Common Origins of Modern Biblical Studies and the Academic Study of Religion," at the American Academy of Religion Annual Meeting, for the Cultural History of the Study of Religion Group, in San Francisco, CA, on November 21, 2011. I later revised that work and published it as, "Secularization, Objectivity, and Enlightenment Scholarship: The Theological and Political Origins of Modern Biblical Studies," in *Logos*. I then revised, expanded, and altered this work, including it in this chapter, with permission, for which I thank *Logos*.

I owe numerous people thanks for their help during the many stages that resulted in this present volume. I thank Scott Hahn and Benjamin Wiker for providing me with early copies of their work, which assisted me in my own, and for the many fruitful conversations on the material in this book. My father, Jay Morrow, also helped critique a draft of what became chapter five. Timothy Furry was the first person to point me to the work of Constantin Fasolt, which I found helpful in this volume. My dissertation director, William Portier, helped me immensely in directing me to the kind of research which I engage in this volume, and has continued to serve as a source of encouragement and inspiration.

Andrew Jones's work, *Before Church and State: A Study of Social Order in St. Louis IX's Sacramental Kingdom*, as well as our many fruitful conversations, has helped me rethink the entire history of secularization. The influence of Jones's work on my thinking can be felt in these pages, but they only resulted in a few revisions. In reality, and had I more time, this entire book could be rewritten—and perhaps it should be—in light of Jones's study. In future works, I intend to build more thoroughly on what Jones has done. Finally, I owe my wife Maria more thanks than I could ever communicate in writing. Not only did she help me in the time-consuming work of revision for the initial articles that make up chapters 2, 4, and 5,

ACKNOWLEDGMENTS

but she also helped me by critiquing a draft of this entire volume. It is to Maria that I dedicate this book.

Introduction

I REMEMBER THE EXAM as if it were yesterday. I sat at the table with the five members of my examination committee. None of them seemed very happy, and I was incredibly nervous. This was my first doctoral exam. At the time that I was going through the doctoral program, four doctoral examinations were required prior to commencing work on the dissertation. The first three, however, were general exams, covering a broad range of topics (e.g., historical, systematic, and moral theology). The fourth exam, which was specific to the program—the "US Catholic experience"—also included the dissertation prospectus. Whereas students were only permitted to take the fourth exam after the satisfactory completion of their doctoral courses, general examinations, and language/research skill requirements—after which they were unofficially referred to as ABD, "all but dissertation"—the first three general exams could be taken, at least back then, whenever a student and their committee chair determined they were ready. I had the nerve to take my first general exam a mere two months into the doctoral program, in the middle of my first semester of doctoral courses.

My first exam was in biblical studies. Our general exams consisted of three parts. For the first part, you were handed two questions and then entered a room with a computer with no internet access and no other resources. You selected one of the two options and then wrote off the cuff within a two-hour time period. After turning in the response, you were handed a second set of two questions for which you had twenty-four hours to complete. This time, you were allowed whatever resources you could find, but you only had twenty-four hours. We knew it could be any one of a dozen or so questions, so I had prepared in advance by placing stacks of relevant biblical studies books and articles on various topics on the floor of my two-bedroom apartment that I shared with a fellow student. After making my choice, I went to the most relevant pile, put the resources near my computer, ordered pizza and a two liter of fully-caffeinated Diet

Coke, and got to work. About twenty-three hours later, only stopping for bathroom breaks, I printed out and turned in my response. I went home, showered, and went to sleep.

The third part of the exam, the oral part, came a week or so later with the members of the five person exam committee, who were not necessarily the same as the eventual dissertation committee. These professors asked questions about the student responses, and, if time remained, about the questions left unanswered. In my case, the majority of the questioning came from my twenty-four hour essay, where I had answered the following: "Explain the history of the development of the Documentary Hypothesis for the origin of the Pentateuch. What are some of the strengths of this hypothesis? What are some of the weaknesses of this hypothesis?" The bulk of what I wrote focused on the history of the development of what would come to be known as the Documentary Hypothesis, made famous by Julius Wellhausen (1844–1918). However, the majority of my oral examination— at least as I remember it—consisted of interrogation of my comments concerning weaknesses of the hypothesis.

I knew and got along well with all five professors; I had, after all, spent the past two years in the master's program there with the same faculty, and I was the one who had selected the individual members of the committee. It included the professor I hoped would (and in fact later did) direct my doctoral dissertation, as well as the professor who had previously directed my master's thesis. Another member of the committee had also served as one of the three readers of my master's thesis. Overall, you would be hard pressed to find a friendlier committee. In fact, a little over a year after I graduated with my doctorate, I would re-enter the department as a full time faculty member with a one year lecturer position, and each of these committee members became my colleagues. I now consider all of them my friends.

And yet, it was somewhat of a difficult experience. At the time, with a number of years still ahead in the program and the serious looks on everyone's faces, I must admit I was more than a little frightened. They were clearly not very happy with what I had identified as weaknesses with the Documentary Hypothesis. One faculty member, more than once, tried to determine if I was really trying to argue that Moses was the author of the Pentateuch, which I made clear was not the argument I had written in my essay. But what I had written there, I thought then and still think now, did make the notion of a more unified author plausible. The reason I include this lengthy anecdote at the beginning of this volume is because of one particular comment made during the oral portion of this exam. I was particularly struck by how one professor compared the work of historical criticism, source criticism in particular, and even more specifically, the Documentary Hypothesis, to nuclear physics. Yes, it may be used for bad ends, suggested the professor, but there is no debating the facts of the science behind it.

I passed the exam, but I was slightly traumatized by the event, which coincided with something else of great significance: immediately after the exam, I was scheduled to have my first phone conversation with a girl I had just met at a friend's wedding the weekend before. Little did I know at the time of the exam that within a few weeks, that girl, Maria, and I would begin dating long distance, we would be engaged to be married less than four months later, she would enter the master's program (and later earn her theology doctorate) the following year, and we would be married less than two years after meeting. Thirteen years of marriage, six children, and many, many conversations on this topic later, I am writing this introduction for a book that I dedicate to her. That this exam happened during this eventful time in my life probably accounts in part for the impression it has left on me. But it also, in part, explains the course of my own scholarship. The Documentary Hypothesis is not akin to nuclear physics. It is not a demonstrative conclusion with mathematic certitude or decisively backed by scientific evidence. Rather, it is, as the term suggests, a literary hypothesis concerning composition. Moreover, it was a hypothesis developed, in part, to serve broader political ends.

Readers who are not specialists in the history of biblical scholarship might wonder why Morrow is writing yet another book covering some of the same terrain as he already did in *Three Skeptics and the Bible* and *Theology, Politics, and Exegesis*. This present volume serves as a sort of third installment in the series, but was another sequel really necessary? The answer is yes. Fifteen years after my exam, I am convinced that this history continues to be underappreciated and yet ever so important. My reasons for this are partly autobiographical, so I hope you readers bear with me as I explain some of the history of my own forays into the history of scholarship.

I entered Miami University in Oxford, Ohio, identifying as a Jewish agnostic with a Zoology major intent on studying human evolution by way of primate biology and behavior. As an undergraduate, I became an evangelical Protestant and then was baptized in the Catholic Church.[1] I

---

1. Part of this story is discussed in Morrow, *Jesus' Resurrection*.

would graduate with a double major in Comparative Religion and Classical Greek and a minor in Jewish Studies. But it was my History course with Edwin Yamauchi, reading his works, and my time spent in his office hours, which were most pivotal for the present discussion.[2] Yamauchi had shown me how, with increasing evidence from the ancient Near East, some of the assured results of modern historical biblical criticism lacked the explanatory power of the traditional Jewish and Christian views they challenged. He then explained how this should not come as any great surprise since a number of these views were developed in a vacuum or, at least, without much—if any—comparison with ancient Near Eastern materials.

Take the controversial issue brought up at the outset of this introduction with my biblical studies doctoral exam, the question of the Pentateuch. Wellhausen consciously ignored materials from the ancient Near East in his formulation of the Documentary Hyopthesis.[3] Scholars like Kenneth Kitchen and James Hoffmeier have made compelling cases for the antiquity (second millennium) and authentic Egyptian context for much of the Pentateuch.[4] Despite the fact that Kitchen and Hoffmeier are world class Egyptologists, they are frequently dismissed as evangelical Protestants and thus biased, as if non-evangelical scholars are unbiased. Such dismissal is more difficult, however, when it comes to non-evangelical scholars, especially Jewish scholars like Joshua Berman, Umberto Cassuto (1883–1951), Yehezkel Kaufmann (1889–1963), Gary Rendsburg, and especially Cyrus Gordon (1908–2001).[5]

Although one could reasonably presume Kitchen, Hoffemeier, and even Berman might hold to the more traditional Mosaic authorship of the Pentateuch, none of these other scholars did. Cassuto thought the Pentateuch was much later, agreeing with Documentarians who placed its final form closer to the time of Ezra, except that Cassuto saw the text as patently unitary. Gordon was a secular Jew, and he had no stake in the debates about authorship. If anything, he was the least affected by religious or related bias in his investigations. Even more difficult to dismiss is Ronald Whybray's

---

2. On Yamauchi, see Calvert, "Edwin M. Yamauchi," 1–23; Yamauchi, "Ancient Historian's View," 192–99.

3. See Machinist, "Road Not Taken," 469–532.

4. See Kitchen, *On the Reliability*; Hoffmeier, *Israel in Egypt*; Hoffmeier, *Ancient Israel in Sinai*.

5. See Berman, "CTH 133," 25–44; Cassuto, *La questione*; Cassuto, *Documentary Hypothesis*; Kaufmann, *Religion of Israel*; Rendsburg, *Redaction of Genesis*; Gordon, "Higher Critics," 131–34.

work, which also dates the Pentateuch much later than was traditionally understood, but like these others, saw the volume as the work of a single primary author.[6] Such studies helped me recognize that scholarship such as modern historical criticism, like all scholarship, was not static but rather evolved and developed. Sometimes hypotheses were abandoned as new evidence and arguments won the day. Sometimes older views were resurrected as they evidenced greater explanatory power over time. But as with many academic disciplines, such changes or paradigm shifts often take time and are frequently resisted by the establishment.[7] This is what Gordon encountered early in the twentieth century:

> While at Dropsie, I reread the description of Utnapishtim's ark in the Gilgamesh Epic and observed a similar concern with detailed specifications. If this feature obliged us to attribute the Genesis account to P of the fifth century, it must, I reasoned, do the same for the Babylonian account, which is absurd. I also found other absurdities in the so-called higher criticism of the Establishment. If *Yahweh-Elohim* owed its origin to the combination of God's name in J . . . with his name in E (*Elohim*), then every Egyptian inscription mentioning the god Amon-Re must have derived the name from an A-document combined with an R-document. One might also argue the same for Ugaritic documents, which abound with divine names composed of two elements. . . . I did not yet fully realize that in any establishment, changes in detail may be tolerated but not the rejection of the system as a whole.[8]

It was only later, in graduate school, that I encountered the then Joseph Cardinal Ratzinger's (now Pope Emeritus Benedict XVI) famous lecture, "Biblical Interpretation in Crisis."[9] Ratzinger challenged the alleged neutrality of modern historical biblical criticism. He noted how much of modern historical biblical criticism styled itself on the hard sciences like physics and chemistry. He underscored how even such hard sciences, however, required a level of involvement and interest on the part of the experimenter; that is, objectivity is unattainable. Claims of objectivity are

---

6. See Whybray, *Making of the Pentateuch*.
7. See Kuhn, *Structure of Scientific*.
8. Gordon, *Scholar's Odyssey*, 80–81.
9. The shorter, English version of his lecture, which he delivered as the Erasmus Lecture (1988) in New York City was published in Ratzinger, "Biblical Interpretation in Crisis," 1–23. Later, lengthier English editions were subsequently published, e.g., Ratzinger, "Biblical Interpretation in Conflict," 91–126.

mere pretensions, indicating the lack of realization of one's biases rather than successful neutrality. Ratzinger's description matched my experience of modern biblical studies both at a public state university and at a private Catholic university, as evidenced by my first Bible exam, with the comparison of the Documentary Hypothesis to nuclear physics. Moreover, my teachers represented the institutions where they had studied the Bible, e.g., Harvard University, the University of Chicago, Vanderbilt University, and the Pontifical Biblical Institute in Rome.

When I entered the doctoral program, I quickly became fascinated by the history of modern biblical studies. In the course of one of my first classes on methods for studying theology, the instructor, William Portier (who later became my dissertation director), had us read John Milbank's controversial tome, *Theology and Social Theory: Beyond Secular Reason*. In Milbank's volume, he had a short subsection entitled, "Modern Politics as Biblical Hermeneutics," wherein he identified Thomas Hobbes (1588–1679) and Baruch Spinoza (1632–1677) as the key figures involved in the transformation of traditional theological biblical interpretation to what would become pre-theological (at best) modern historical biblical criticism.[10] Moreover, as the title of his subsection communicated, such biblical studies became politically motivated—at least in part. Milbank argued that politics affected and shaped modern biblical scholarship in its infancy.

I was stunned. It was as if scales fell off my eyes. Now, I began to understand part of the *reason* why some of the views with diminishing explanatory power emerged in the first place, and why they survived. Regardless of their veracity or even the reach of their explanatory power, some of the very methods themselves were constructed with theo-political purposes or, at least in part, as political tools. Hence Hobbes and Spinoza, two pioneering architects of such methods, were primarily thought of as political theorists. The following year, I took one of Portier's courses, entitled "God and the State," on the interface of theology and politics from the Reformation onward. For my research, Portier suggested I examine this history in light of the history of early modern politics that we were studying, so I did. By this time, I had encountered Jon Levenson's famous essay, "Historical Criticism and the Fate of the Enlightenment Project," republished in his *The Hebrew Bible, the Old Testament, and Historical Criticism*.[11] Levenson linked Hobbes, Spinoza, and Fr. Richard Simon (1638–1712) as the three

---

10. See Milbank, *Theology and Social Theory*, 18–22.
11. See Levenson, *Hebrew Bible*, 106–26.

key pioneers of modern historical biblical criticism—the discipline in which he is justly recognized as a foremost practitioner. I thus decided to study those three figures myself.

I quickly realized I had bitten off more than I could chew for a semester's research paper and instead limited my work to Hobbes. That paper went through numerous iterations after my two drafts for Portier: in 2007, I presented a version of it at the Society of Biblical Literature; in 2011, a revised version was published in *Christianity & Literature*; and another revised version became the third chapter of my first book, *Three Skeptics and the Bible*.[12] All that remained, or so I naively thought, was to study Spinoza and Simon. After completing my doctoral course work and exams, I was awarded a research grant to study Spinoza. Maria and I were married about two weeks after my qualifying exam, and on the coattails of our honeymoon, we spent nearly two months in Jerusalem as visiting research scholars at Tantur Ecumenical Institute, both of us funded by grants from the University of Dayton, which made such a trip possible.

In Jerusalem, while commencing work on my doctoral dissertation—which I had informally begun upon entering the doctoral program two years prior, under Portier's tutelage—I worked on my grant project concerning the political background of Spinoza's early foundational work in modern historical biblical criticism. I had met Scott Hahn, whose work had helped immensely in my conversion to Catholicism as an undergraduate, the year before. Hahn's work was the focus of my doctoral dissertation, "Evangelical Catholics and Catholic Biblical Scholarship: An Examination of Scott Hahn's Canonical, Liturgical, and Covenantal Biblical Exegesis."[13] Such a topic fit perfectly in a program on the US Catholic experience, as well as with my interests in biblical interpretation, and my own autobiography. Hahn and I discovered we were kindred spirits and became fast friends despite the complications of his being the focus of my study. When I met him, Hahn was already collaborating with Benjamin Wiker on a massive volume which would become their *Politicizing the Bible: The Roots of Historical Criticism and the Secularization of Scripture 1300–1700*, and he put me in contact with Wiker, who was working on Spinoza as I was.[14] He helped point me to useful sources for my work, and I, too, helped point him to some useful sources for

---

12. See Morrow, *Three Skeptics and the Bible*, 85–103.
13. See Morrow, "Evangelical Catholics."
14. See Hahn and Wiker, *Politicizing the Bible*.

theirs. My correspondence with Hahn and Wiker helped me think through many of the issues I was working on.

Hahn paved the way for much of this research in his published interview, which later became a book chapter, "The Bible Politicized: The Roots and Fruits of Historical Criticism."[15] Through my correspondence with Hahn and Wiker, I quickly became aware that the roots of what we were uncovering were far deeper than merely Hobbes and Spinoza but rather reached back into the medieval period. I became overwhelmed with the research I was uncovering, as each historical author seemed to point backward to a previous one. I decided to focus on the seventeenth century, since that is where I began and because the work of scholars during that period was so pivotal a shift from what came before, even as it built upon prior work.

Ratzinger's clarion call in his "Biblical Interpretation in Crisis" was for a critical examination of historical criticism, uncovering its historical roots and philosophical presuppositions in order better to understand its limits, but also its positive and constructive abilities. His hope was to develop a method combining the best of both traditional theological methods and the pre-theological methods of modern historical biblical criticism.[16] He demonstrated the sort of work which he called for in his *Jesus of Nazareth* trilogy.[17] I have taken his methodological project as the starting point of my own work, and this book aims at a further contribution toward a criticism of biblical criticism. I hope to continue to challenge the pretensions of objectivity assumed by so much of the discipline of modern biblical studies. The goal of such a project is to create a space where modern biblical criticism can be evaluated properly so that its best gains can bear fruit, while the Bible can again be approached as the theological wellspring it is intended to be.

In the first chapter, I take a broad look at the history of modern biblical criticism from the fourteenth century through the Protestant Reformation. The focus is on different political and philosophical contexts at various stages, looking at the major figures with which Hahn and Wiker begin their *Politicizing the Bible*: Marsilius of Padua (1275–1342), William of Ockham (1285–1347), John Wycliffe (1330–1384), Niccolò Machiavelli (1469–1527), and Martin Luther (1483–1546), concluding with

---

15. See Hahn, *Scripture Matters*, 137–58.
16. See Stallsworth, "Story of an Encounter," 102–90.
17. See Benedict XVI, *Jesus of Nazareth I–III*.

the English Reformation of Henry VIII. In the second chapter, I return to the key seventeenth-century figures I examined in *Three Skeptics and the Bible*, namely, Isaac La Peyrère (1596–1676), Hobbes, and Spinoza. This much briefer treatment represents a significant advancement over what I wrote in *Three Skeptics and the Bible*, based upon my continued research on these three pivotal figures.

In the third chapter, I come back to the broader approach of the first chapter, situating the seventeenth-century work of Hobbes, Spinoza, and Simon—whom I discussed in *Theology, Politics, and Exegesis*[18]—in the context of the other important seventeenth-century figures Hahn and Wiker discuss in *Politicizing the Bible*: René Descartes (1596–1650), John Locke (1632–1704), and John Toland (1670–1722). The fourth chapter focuses on the changing notions of biblical inspiration implied in the history of biblical interpretation from antiquity through the Roman Catholic Modernist crisis at the dawn of the twentieth century. Here, I show how the challenges posed by modern biblical criticism as it entered the Catholic world more widely triggered the official Catholic responses to such criticism and Catholic reflection on inspiration. Finally, the fifth chapter looks at the quest for objectivity within biblical studies in the context of secularization.

---

18. See Morrow, *Theology, Politics, and Exegesis*, 35–51.

1

Back to the Source

Biblical Criticism in the Renaissance and Reformation

THE TASK OF THIS first chapter is to provide an overview of the political and philosophical background to the history of modern biblical criticism from the fourteenth century through the Reformation. The chapter expands upon the first chapter in my previous book, *Theology, Politics, and Exegesis*.[1] In particular, it elaborates upon the role of Marsilus of Padua (1275-1342) and William of Ockham (1285-1347) through the period of the Protestant Reformation.[2] As with that volume, this book follows the basic outline Scott Hahn and Benjamin Wiker constructed in their *Politicizing the Bible: The Roots of Historical Criticism and the Secularization of Scripture 1300-1700*, with which I am in substantial agreement.[3] Their introductory chapter helpfully sets the stage for the history that follows, and this is a valuable contribution.

As their subtitle—"The Secularization of Scripture"—indicates, these authors underscore some of the ways in which the interpretation and study of Scripture has been secularized over the course of centuries. Far too rarely in brief surveys of biblical scholarship has the role of politics and philosophy been addressed, let alone addressed adequately. Hahn and Wiker demonstrate how various political concerns and undergirding

---

1. See Morrow, *Theology, Politics, and Exegesis*, 1–15.
2. See Morrow, *Theology, Politics, and Exegesis*, 1–8.
3. See Hahn and Wiker, *Politicizing the Bible*. The first chapter of *Theology, Politics, and Exegesis* originated as a lengthy, thirteen-page review of their volume in Morrow, "Untold History," 145–55. The present chapter, in this new volume, originated in the first half of a much more lengthy, forty-seven-page review essay of their volume in Morrow, "Averroism, Nominalism, and Mechanization," 1293–340. In this volume, chapter 3 will be based on the second half of this essay.

philosophies shaped and guided the long process which led to the historical critical method of biblical interpretation. They situate this process within the broader historical, political, philosophical, and theological contexts in which historical criticism was formed. Moreover, they situate the contributions of the major figures involved in this process within the context of their biographies, which proves to be so necessary for understanding this history. Hahn and Wiker consider an expansive and often neglected period within the history of modern biblical criticism.[4] I have tried to contribute to this project through my *Three Skeptics and the Bible*,[5] my sequel to that volume, *Theology, Politics, and Exegesis*, and now, with the present, third installment in that series.

Following Hahn and Wiker's outline, as well as the initial sketch I made at the beginning of *Theology, Politics, and Exegesis*, I begin this chapter by showing how Marsilius of Padua's and William of Ockham's arguments justify the subordination of the church to the state. Hahn and Wiker suggested this had to do with Marsilius's Averroist philosophical underpinnings and Ockham's nominalism. As we shall see, however, it is not certain that Marsilius was an Averroist. Regardless, such Averroist and nominalist philosophies continued to undergird much of the future of historical critical exegesis, even if these may not have been the sole or primary driving forces with Marsilius and Ockham.

After this, I turn to Wycliffe's attack upon nominalism and how it inadvertently supported the same sort of exegesis and subordination of the church to the state as had Marsilius and Ockham. Thus, for theological reasons (and for philosophical reasons, directly opposed to Ockham) Wycliffe brought to English and—through his followers—to German soil the subordination of the church to the state, as Marsilius and Ockham had argued. Thus, the foundation was set for the German and English Reformations which would soon follow. Next, I turn to Machiavelli, showing how Machiavelli created a hermeneutic of suspicion, where, much like Averroës, he saw religion as a veil for more crafty political machinations of hypocritical rulers.

---

4. For brief, article-length overviews likewise emphasizing the political history moving from the medieval period into the nineteenth century, overlapping with some of the figures they study (Marsilius, Ockham, Machiavelli, Hobbes, Spinoza, and Simon), see chapters 4–5 in this present volume and Morrow, *Theology, Politics, and Exegesis*, 10–53, 74–90.

5. Morrow, *Three Skeptics and the Bible*.

From Machiavelli, I turn to Luther and the Protestant Reformation, where we find Luther and his co-Reformers inspired in part by the widespread corruption among clerical leaders within the Catholic hierarchy. Luther was a nominalist and self-identified as a follower of Ockham. Luther built upon the groundwork laid by Marsilius and Wycliffe, and he inadvertently aided in the transformation of the public civic realm into a secular realm, wherein the state controlled the church. After Luther, I conclude with the English Reformation of King Henry VIII, showing how his reforming policy built upon all the influential figures whom I have previously discussed: Marsilius, directly through Henry's advisors; Ockham, implied through the German Protestant influence; Wycliffe, through the influence of English Lollardy, which had so shaped English nationalist aspirations as well as prepare the groundwork in Germany for the Reformation; Machiavelli, directly through Henry's advisors; and Luther, through embracing the Protestant Reforming agenda in England.

In Hahn and Wiker's volume, their overarching argument is that "the development of the historical-critical method in biblical studies is only fully intelligible as part of the more comprehensive project of secularization that occurred in the West over the last seven hundred years, and that the politicizing of the Bible was, in one way or another, essential to this project."[6] In roughly the first half of their volume, Hahn and Wiker show how the stage is set for the drama of historical criticism's evolution. In the second half of the text, the authors illustrate how specific exegetes operated within the intellectual and political world created by the figures discussed in the first half.

I would modify Hahn and Wiker's claim only slightly, in order to accommodate an important insight found in Andrew Jones's important work, *Before Church and State*. Jones has shown how problematic it is to read church and state conflicts back into the medieval period; this is an anachronistic viewpoint influenced by our own contemporary experience of church and state.[7] In the medieval period, the secular was not what we take it to mean today (more on this in chapter five). Church and state were not vying for political authority, contrary to the many studies by revered historians of the past more than a century. In fact, church and state, as two completely

---

6. Hahn and Wiker, *Politicizing the Bible*, 8. They explain that, "By politicization, we mean the *intentional exegetical reinterpretation of Scripture so as to make it serve a merely political, this worldly (hence secular) goal*" (Hahn and Wiker, *Politicizing the Bible*, 9).

7. See Jones, *Before Church and State*.

separable institutions, did not exist in the world of medieval Christendom. Instead, lay and ecclesiastical rulers saw themselves as enmeshed in the same sacramental world—fulfilling different roles, but working together for a common goal, both earthly and heavenly, directed at temporal peace and eternal beatitude.

I would thus rephrase Hahn and Wiker's quotation to something like this: "the development of the historical-critical method in biblical studies is only fully intelligible as part of" a more complicated, seven-hundred-year history of developments in biblical exegesis. In the latter part of this history, historical biblical criticism formed "a part of the more comprehensive project of secularization that occurred in the West." "The politicizing of the Bible was, in one way or another, essential to this project."

Pretensions of Historical Criticism

We can begin by calling into question the objective neutrality of the historical critical method; it has never been disinterested and neutral, nor was it always articulated as such.[8] Although it is commonplace in textbook accounts of historical-criticism to see the method as a product of the nineteenth century, increasingly, scholars identify the roots of historical criticism in the eighteenth and seventeenth centuries. The roots are far deeper; we can extend the historical-critical genealogical tree at least into the fourteenth century, at the end of the medieval period, but probably much earlier. Hahn and Wiker explain that: "The late-eighteenth-century Enlightenment is not the beginning of the conflict, but the culmination of several centuries of a slowly-building, new, . . . secular worldview."[9] I would again modify their claim. What we typically identify as the Enlightenment did in fact build slowly on top of what came before, but not all of the stages were secularizing in the modern sense. Marsilius's work, for example, could fit within traditional Christian notions of how politics should function within Christendom.

These points notwithstanding, the roots of historical-criticism and modern politics are linked, e.g., in figures such as Marsilius, Machiavelli, Hobbes, Spinoza, and Locke. In addition, the Enlightenment's

---

8. In what follows, see Hahn and Wiker, *Politicizing the Bible*, 1–16.

9. They include a parenthetical explanation bringing attention to the role of the comma in this sentence: "It's not a new secular as opposed to the old secular" (Hahn and Wiker, *Politicizing the Bible*, 7).

increasingly secular political agenda works through the historical-critical method through the nineteenth century and beyond. Ernst Troeltsch's programmatic discussion of such a method—wherein the supernatural is systematically excluded—serves as a case in point. Hahn and Wiker explain the impact of this: "In doing so, it removes Christianity as a political force, making of it at best a bearer of nondogmatic moral teachings that undergird the political order."[10] What is significant here is that the guiding presuppositions of methods like Troeltsch's pre-determine how modern biblical interpreters use history. What is unique to modern historical biblical criticism is not the various scholarly tools of textual criticism, philology, archaeology, etc., that it employs. Rather, in Hahn and Wiker's words: "This union of tools with secularizing presuppositions constitutes what is almost invariably meant by the historical-critical method."[11]

The Poverty Dispute: The Contributions of Marsilius and Ockham

The first clear stage we must discuss is with Marsilius and Ockham.[12] The historical backdrop is that of the Avignon Papacy, without which it is difficult to understand Marsilius's and Ockham's discussions of Scripture. Within this broader context, one issue which loomed large in the background was the debate concerning Franciscan poverty. The question revolved around religious ownership and use among the Franciscans. Franciscans, like members of other religious orders, took vows of poverty. Poverty perhaps typified the Franciscan charism more so than other orders, and yet, Franciscans found themselves in need of books for teaching, preaching, and study. Books, in turn, needed to be housed somewhere, which implied the use of libraries. How could the apparent possession and use of often quite expensive material items such as books, lavish buildings, and land for libraries be reconciled with the evangelical counsel of poverty as vowed by Franciscans?

Popes Gregory IX (reigned 1227–1241), Nicholas III (reigned 1277–1280), and Clement V (1305–1314), had allowed the Franciscans to distinguish their use from ownership. The idea some Franciscans proposed was that the papacy owned the temporal items and land that the Franciscans

10. Hahn and Wiker, *Politicizing the Bible*, 11.
11. Hahn and Wiker, *Politicizing the Bible*, 12.
12. For what follows, see Hahn and Wiker, *Politicizing the Bible*, 17–59.

merely used. This notion was backed by the papacy for a while—at least under Nicholas—but things soon began to change under a later pope. Pope John XXII (reigned 1316–1334) challenged this understanding by denying the papacy's ownership of any of the things the Franciscans were using; he denied their distinction between use and ownership.

So-called Conventual Franciscans tried to live in poverty while using the things of the world to fulfill whatever obligations they had. The so-called Spiritual Franciscans desired reform, understanding the Conventuals to be living a more luxurious lifestyle unbecoming of a religious person, let alone a Franciscan. Franciscan leadership was held among the Conventuals, who demanded the Spirituals fall in line and obey. John XXII likewise exhorted the Spirituals to obedience. In demurring against the idea of papal ownership for that which Franciscans used, however, John XXII came into conflict with the Conventuals, who used that distinction to support their practice.

As this conflict with the Franciscans over poverty was raging, John XXII and Ludwig of Bavaria were in a separate conflict that soon became embroiled in the poverty dispute. Rival political factions had thrown their support for different rulers of the Germanic realm. Some supported Frederick I, whereas others supported Ludwig. The dispute became intractable, thus John XXII intervened, asking both potential rulers to abdicate. In the meantime, John XXII proposed that he would reign—as pope—until another ruler could be found.

Ludwig declared Pope John XXII a heretic when the pope's decision regarding Franciscan poverty differed from Nicholas V, his earlier predecessor. Thus, the Franciscan poverty debate became a political means of Ludwig challenging the papacy of John XXII.[13] This does not mean that Ludwig was opposed to the Church or the authority of the pope, as Jones's work with the thirteenth century has shown. It is clear, however, that Ludwig thought he should rule the Germanic realm and that the pope was overstepping his authority by intervening in the Franciscan dispute. At the same time, it should be recalled that the papal court of Avignon lived at a level of luxury that was scandalous, and this likely added insult to the Spirituals' challenge. Michael of Cesena, the Franciscan Minister General, would have been gratified by Pope John XXII's demand that the

---

13. For further background to this debate over Franciscan poverty in the context of debates about papal authority and infallibility, see Heft, *John XXII*; Tierney, *Origins of Papal Infallibility*.

Spiritual Franciscans obey their rightful authorities. Michael of Cesena, however, along with the rest of the Conventual Franciscans, was incensed with Pope John's denial that the Franciscans merely used things which were the property of the papacy and his denial of the papacy's ownership of the things the Franciscans used.

Marsilius and Ockham thus found themselves in the very middle of these controversies. Both resided under Ludwig of Bavaria's protection when they came into conflict with Pope John XXII. Hahn and Wiker argued that Marsilius was likely steeped in the medieval-Muslim, Averroist philosophy so prevalent at the University of Padua in his day. This claim is certainly plausible, but, at the same time, it is unnecessary to explain his most important political work, which they consider his *Defensor Pacis*. Ibn Rushd, known in the West as Averroës, was a significant Muslim philosopher whose commentaries on Aristotle became widely influential in the Medieval world.

Averroës's work was received in the Latin Christian West in such a way as to be understood as an attempt to respond to apparent inconsistencies between the Qur'an and Aristotle's thought. Averroës argued that truth can be recognized and understood differently by different people. The differences lay in the various levels of ability or different capacities of those seeking to recognize or understand the truth. Averroës placed philosophers at the top rung within this schematic hierarchy. In the Latin West, this notion, labelled "Averroist," implied the "superiority of the truths of natural reason to those of revelation."[14] This characterization led to the so-called double truth approach of the Latin Averroist tradition. This Latin Averroism found an important home at the University of Padua, from whence it spread throughout Europe. If Marsilius was in fact Averroist, as Hahn and Wiker maintain, then he likely became Averroist while studying at Padua or perhaps later, when he served as rector at the University of Paris, which was also a major center of Averroist thought.

One of Marsilius's most influential works was his political treatise *Defensor Pacis*, an anti-papal work he completed in 1324. Marsilius's treatise was "revolutionary, a landmark philosophical document in the secularization of the West."[15] When considering *Defensor Pacis* as coming from an Averroist perspective (as Hahn and Wiker read it), one can see Marsilius's politics were grounded in reason, separated from faith. This is not the only

14. Hahn and Wiker, *Politicizing the Bible*, 23.
15. Hahn and Wiker, *Politicizing the Bible*, 25.

way to read *Defensor Pacis*, however. If we take Jones's argument in *Before Church and State* seriously, we could read *Defensor Pacis* as one legitimate Christian articulation of the relationship between temporal and ecclesiastical rulers that fits within Christendom. Although Marsilius's primary concern in his treatise appears to be the attempt to secure civil peace, this does not have to be viewed as his ultimate goal.

Hahn and Wiker explain: "Although Marsilius is evidently concerned with undermining papal authority in the political realm, his ultimate concern is the radical reordering of secular and sacred authority, so that the priesthood is firmly subordinated to political power."[16] This is a convincing argument, and I incorporated it into *Three Skeptics and the Bible*.[17] However, Jones's *Before Church and State* complicates the historical context, implying that this might not be the best reading of Marsilius. It is probably true, as Hahn and Wiker point out, that Marsilius was relying upon Aristotle filtered through Averroës to make his case, since Averroës would have been one of the main commentators on Aristotle that would have been available to him. It may also be true, as they argue, that this might have been a "truncated view" of Aristotle's thicker description of politics.[18] In light of the late-medieval context of his work, however, it may still be the case that his ordering of temporal and ecclesiastical authorities fit within a shared conception of the "business of the peace and the faith," as Jones explains society in thirteenth-century France.[19]

Thus, I no longer think it is so clear that Marsilius's use of the Bible in *Defensor Pacis* "serves the secularizing aim of Marsilius's politics."[20] That is, Hahn and Wiker argue that Marsilius used Scripture, but only when he was able to distort its interpretation in the service of his secular ends. Could it not be that his focus on temporal authorities served the "business of the peace and faith" in a way that would have been viewed as a legitimate option in medieval Christendom prior to the Protestant Reformation? Both are plausible readings of Marsilius's work. If we take Marsilius at his word, he does fit within his medieval context. What is clear is that the sorts of comments he makes regarding temporal authorities match later post-Enlightenment, secularizing trends that are widespread and come to dominate

16. Hahn and Wiker, *Politicizing the Bible*, 26.
17. See my comments in Morrow, *Three Skeptics and the Bible*, 18–19.
18. Hahn and Wiker, *Politicizing the Bible*, 28.
19. See Jones, *Before Church and State*, 31–36.
20. Hahn and Wiker, *Politicizing the Bible*, 29.

the West. In the end, Marsilius did envision that temporal authorities would play an authoritative role in biblical interpretation, but perhaps not quite as totalizing as Thomas Hobbes (1588–1679) would later articulate.

As with later, more secularized approaches, Marsilius deemed it important that the temporal rulers would exercise some control over church offices. This need not be interpreted as Marsilius's ploy to have temporal rulers control Church decisions, but it certainly could be used that way, and later, in the seventeenth century and beyond, such arguments would be used precisely as such. Marsilius also articulated what might be viewed as an early form of *sola Scriptura*, where the Bible functioned as sole authority over and against tradition. For Marsilius, however, it was not a Bible left to individual interpretation but rather a Bible interpreted correctly by the authoritative exegetes appointed by temporal rulers.

For Marsilius, the Old Testament no longer had an authoritative position for Christians. He further argued for recourse to the literal sense alone, eschewing any spiritual sense of Scripture. In part, it appears Marsilius may have rejected spiritual interpretation because of how such interpretations were used to support the temporal authority of the papacy. It should be obvious that Marsilius intended *Defensor Pacis* to serve as a practical means of quelling papal claims to temporal rule, placing such temporal rule solely in the hands of lay rulers; he never intended his treatise to be merely theoretical. Thus, it should not come as any surprise that Marsilius joined the side of those Franciscans opposing Pope John XXII; after all, John XXII had argued for a papal role in temporal rule of the Germanic realm, asserting that he should rule the kingdom until their new ruler was established. As Hahn and Wiker explain, "Arguing on behalf of the absolute poverty of Christ and the Apostles through appeal to the New Testament, Marsilius sought to strip the papacy of temporal power."[21]

Ockham eventually joined Marsilius under Ludwig of Bavaria's protection. As a Franciscan concerned over the poverty dispute, Ockham's arguments were more spiritual in nature than Marsilius's and less concerned with the ordering of temporal society. John XXII was upset with Ockham's arguments, so Ockham fled with the head of his order, Michael of Cesena, to Ludwig's protection, under which Ockham wrote against John XXII. Hahn and Wiker observe that: "Unlike Marsilius, Ockham does not subordinate

---

21. Hahn and Wiker, *Politicizing the Bible*, 37. Their sentence concludes with: "So that a secular ruler could establish a purely secular rule," but I think this may overreach the evidence. I am not so sure it was "purely" secular rule they wished to establish, nor "secular" in the modern sense of the word.

the ecclesiastical powers to the political powers; rather, he attempts to reinstate, against later papal pretensions, the generally accepted medieval view that the sacred and the secular are two distinct powers."[22] Ockham argued for the importance of temporal rulers having potential authority over ecclesiastical rulers who might be sinful, and he saw this as more than a merely theoretical argument. For Ockham, the Church was in very real need of reform, as evidenced by the pope's challenge to Franciscan poverty.

When it came to matters of biblical interpretation, Ockham argued for the need of biblical *periti* (experts), or specialists, who would have authority in matters of biblical exegesis. Ockham would not be the last to make such an argument; this notion would play out in very specific ways throughout the later history of biblical interpretation, particularly in the Enlightenment period. For Ockham, however, the biblical expert has more authority over biblical interpretation than Catholic tradition, more even than council or pope.

The question of whether or not Ockham was really nominalist is more complicated than we can treat adequately here. Ockham did appear to deny the existence of universals, which is nominalist. For Ockham, God's will was somewhat arbitrary, a notion which stands in contrast to much of the Latin Averroist tradition. No limit can be placed on God's will since Ockham would see that as a violation of God's absolute sovereignty. Ockham subtly mathematized rationality, at least in a provisional way, and this would pave the way for Descartes later on. Hahn and Wiker note how Descartes filled the vacuum Ockham left in his denial of universals; Descartes "would substitute mathematical forms as the new universals."[23] As with Marsilius, Ockham too focused on the literal sense. Marsilius's and Ockham's notion of a literal sense, however, stood in contrast to how St. Thomas Aquinas (1225–1274) employed it. By a literal reading of Scripture, Marsilius and Ockham appeared to imply something closer to author intent, and that much like other human works of literature.[24]

---

22. Hahn and Wiker, *Politicizing the Bible*, 40.

23. Hahn and Wiker, *Politicizing the Bible*, 52.

24. Aquinas, on the other hand, grounded his understanding on the doctrine of analogy, which emphasized the relationship between created realities and the Creator of those realities. Hahn and Wiker explain: "Both human beings and God can signify according to the historical or literal sense, but only God, properly speaking, can signify in the spiritual sense, for only He can create real things that signify other things.... God wrote allegories into creation itself" (Hahn and Wiker, *Politicizing the Bible*, 55). On Aquinas's biblical interpretation—especially his understanding of the literal sense—see

Wycliffe's Inadvertent Secularization of Biblical Interpretation

John Wycliffe (1330–1384) represents a significant but often ignored pre-Reformation exegete who contributed to the rise of modern biblical criticism.[25] Wycliffe's metaphysical realism provided the foundation for his exegetical program, which was both theological and political. Although Wycliffe was no fan of nominalism and, in fact, an opponent of Ockham's followers, he was equally concerned with Church corruption. Wycliffe forcefully argued that the lay temporal rulers were obliged to control the temporal sphere, much as Marsilius and Ockham had argued earlier. Thus, Wycliffe maintained that such temporal rulers should wield authority over the Church's temporal holdings, including land. As Hahn and Wiker explain, for Wycliffe, "reform of the sacred could only be achieved if the Church's riches and temporal power were taken away by the civil secular sword."[26] It is thus perhaps predictable that Wycliffe's "works received a ready hearing among those in the royal court, for the king had every desire to control and divert payments flowing from England toward Avignon."[27]

In a number of Wycliffe's works—particularly *De Dominio Divino*, *De Civili Dominio*, and *De Officio Regis*—Wycliffe argues for the temporal rulers to disendow the Church of its temporal holdings. For Wycliffe, God granted dominion "on condition that the one exercising dominion is righteous."[28] Wycliffe thus distinguished between civil dominion and what he called "evangelical" dominion, which would function for Wycliffe much as Luther's notion of two kingdoms would function later in the Protestant Reformation. Wycliffe argued, grounded in the discussion in his works, that: "The king can and should take away possessions of ecclesiastics if they are misusing them, or if the possessions themselves are inordinate, on the grounds that the unrighteous have no right of

---

Aquinas, *Summa Theologiae* I.1.10; Aquinas, *Quaestiones disputatae de potentia*, 4.1; Aquinas, *In psalmos Davidis expositio*, prooemium; Boyle, "Authorial Intention," 3–8; Torrell, *Initiation à saint Thomas d'Aquin*, 41–45, 84–85.

25. For what follows on Wycliffe, see Hahn and Wiker, *Politicizing the Bible*, 61–115.
26. Hahn and Wiker, *Politicizing the Bible*, 66.
27. Hahn and Wiker, *Politicizing the Bible*, 66. Although Hahn and Wiker also note: "The English king did not want papal subsidies and tithes to cease since, in practice, they were collected by royal officials who skimmed off half to three-quarters for the royal treasury" (Hahn and Wiker, *Politicizing the Bible*, 66n17).
28. Hahn and Wiker, *Politicizing the Bible*, 66.

dominion—and further because disendowing the clergy returns them to their proper condition of Christ-like poverty."[29]

Wycliffe's *De Veritate Sacrae Scripturae* is particularly helpful for understanding his proposal for biblical interpretation better. In Wycliffe's thought, Jesus, not the biblical texts, is the ultimate word of God; the Bible is thus informed by the Word (Jesus) but is not the Word itself. Wycliffe understood his metaphysical realist approach to be a basic requirement for any biblical interpretation. Wycliffe's comments concerning the forceful removal of the Church's control of temporal matters, including lands, flowed from his philosophy, and it was this philosophy, combined with his concern for the ecclesiastical corruption he observed, that added strength to his arguments.

It is from this broader context that we can better understand Wycliffe's fierce critique of religious life in general—and monastic life in particular. Religious orders, particularly monasteries, held a significant amount of land, which Wycliffe saw as an example of ecclesiastical corruption; the vowed poor living in apparent luxury. For all of his differences with Ockham, we can see a similarity here. Wycliffe served as a "court theologian," and he argued that such court theologians were necessary to curb corruption in the Church. Court theologians would assist the lay temporal rulers in their role of reforming ecclesiastical authority structures. Hahn and Wiker describe Wycliffe's position thus: "The unsheathed sword of the temporal power is not merely for punishing thieves, murderers, etc. but also (among other things) to keep the clergy from grasping at the temporal sword or inordinate temporal holdings."[30]

Wycliffe's radical views were dispersed widely and helped prepare the soil for what would come in the Protestant Reformation and then later, in modern biblical criticism. Scholars often overplay the importance of the so-called Wycliffite Bible, as if it represented a revolutionary attempt to bring the Bible into the vernacular. The translation of Scripture into the vernacular (of which the Wycliffite Bible was not the first) was not so novel but rather part of a much larger transformation of England's culture, involving the transition—more generally—from French to English. Wycliffe almost certainly did not in fact translate the Wycliffite Bible; rather, it was completed by scholars sharing Wycliffe's views.

---

29. Hahn and Wiker, *Politicizing the Bible*, 67.
30. Hahn and Wiker, *Politicizing the Bible*, 93.

In the end, Wycliffe's theological and philosophical notions continued to spread, especially among Bohemian transplants to England who arrived on English soil during the reign of King Richard II after he married Queen Ann of Bohemia. It was in Bohemia that Wycliffe's thought exerted perhaps its most pronounced influence on Jan Hus (1369–1415) and his many followers. The followers of Wycliffe in England came to be known as the Lollards, whereas the followers of Hus in Bohemia were known as Hussites. Both groups, however, began violent revolutions, and they were thus suppressed within both realms. Since Wycliffe and Hus had opposed nominalism, nominalist philosophy was used in attacking Hussite heretical theology. Ironically as it may seem, since Wycliffe had attacked nominalist and Ockhamist thought, Wycliffe unintentionally strengthened arguments concerning temporal rulers that Ockham (and Marsilius) had put forward.[31] This would play an important role in what would soon come in the English Reformation.

Machiavelli's Hermeneutic of Suspicion

From Wycliffe, we now turn to Niccolò Machiavelli (1469–1527), a figure almost universally ignored in histories of modern biblical scholarship.[32] In order to understand Machiavelli's political works, it is important to have some basic knowledge of his immediate context in fifteenth-century Florence. His historical and political works are where his influence in modern biblical criticism may be detected, and this is particularly so with regard to the hermeneutic of suspicion that he creates. His own historical context includes important examples of corruption at the highest levels of the Catholic Church, including the papacy itself, and this proves important for understanding what Machiavelli was about.[33] Hahn and Wiker confess: "In view of the notorious doings of the papacy and Church hierarchy during this period, religious hypocrisy had gone from being a scandal to an art. The

---

31. See Hahn and Wiker, *Politicizing the Bible*, 113, where they conclude: "Although Wycliffe was a declared enemy of Ockham, insofar as he set forth an almost Marsilian argument, he had the unintended effect (as did Ockham) of reinforcing the secularizing, politicizing thrust of Marsilius's thought."

32. For what follows on Machiavelli, see Hahn and Wiker, *Politicizing the Bible*, 117–146.

33. On this, see not only Hahn and Wiker's discussion (Hahn and Wiker, *Politicizing the Bible*, 118–23) but also Duffy, *Saints & Sinners*, 177–215; Kelly, *Oxford Dictionary of Popes*, 250–58; and more recently, Aquilina, *Good Pope, Bad Pope*, 100–110.

damage done to the faith of the Church by the popes during Machiavelli's lifetime is incalculable."[34] One author described the papacy of Machiavelli's age as "a folly of perversity."[35]

Machiavelli had firsthand knowledge of clerical hypocrisy, including among his contemporary popes. In his own works, he universalized this hypocrisy, applying it to all religious leaders, everywhere and at all times. He thus read such dissembling back into ancient texts like the Pentateuch, and assumed figures such as Moses were religious dissemblers as well, using religion for their own political gain. That is, Machiavelli "assumes that all religion of any type is a façade for power."[36] In contrast to how we might take this, Machiavelli did not view all such hypocrisy negatively, but rather thought it was the mark of a good—that is, politically effective—ruler. Machiavelli proposes Pope Alexander VI (reigned 1492–1503) as a prime example of what a politically effective dissembling prince should be like.

Machiavelli wrote his most famous political work, *The Prince*, after he was imprisoned and tortured, the experiences of which almost certainly had an effect on his work. Even prior to his imprisonment, Machiavelli had broad political experience. He had been a Florentine secretary. He had also been officially delegated to represent Florence in political matters and had a number of interactions in that capacity with Pope Alexander VI's "ambitious and ruthless son,"[37] Cesare Borgia (1475–1507). Machiavelli also attempted to form an effective army for Florence, in contrast to the ineffective ones which preceded his time. He spent time in the Germanic realm representing Florence to the Holy Roman Emperor Maximilian I (reigned as Holy Roman Emperor 1493–1519). But perhaps his greatest first-hand political education came from his time as a diplomat for Florence, travelling with Pope Julius II (reigned 1503–1513) while the pope was engaged in battle.

Machiavelli's *The Prince* and his *Discourses on Livy* are both important for understanding the development of a hermeneutic of suspicion in later modern biblical criticism. Machiavelli hoped *The Prince* would shift his contemporary political scene from an ancient model to what would become a modern model. He intended this transformation to leave behind the otherworldly goal envisioned by ancient politics. For Machiavelli, the

---

34. Hahn and Wiker, *Politicizing the Bible*, 118.
35. The quotation is from Tuchman, *March of Folly*, 52.
36. Hahn and Wiker, *Politicizing the Bible*, 122.
37. Hahn and Wiker, *Politicizing the Bible*, 124.

focus should now be only on the present world, where the "goal is the preservation of power."[38] In Hahn and Wiker's words, "Machiavelli's *Prince* is . . . the manual by which one unlearns Plato's *Republic*."[39] Machiavelli's goal, of course, was much broader than this. He sought to secularize all politics for the purpose of a merely earthly peace. To this end, Machiavelli effects "a fundamental shift in the treatment of Scripture."[40] Machiavelli thus places the Moses of the Bible within the context of Greco-Roman political rulers, which basically secularized Moses's position in the Pentateuch. At Machiavelli's hands, we should no longer envision Moses as a prophetic figure who God called to lead his people Israel; rather, in Machiavelli's new exegesis, Moses is transformed into a "merely political leader."[41]

Machiavelli may have written his political history the way he did under the inspiration of the Roman historian Plutarch (46–120). Machiavelli was convinced that the biblical account needed a "corrective." Machiavelli thought that the biblical account of Moses, in stark contrast to Plutarch's histories:

> does not appear to be the result of a careful sifting of multiple views of the same events but presents itself simply as reporting what happened to Moses and the Israelites in their escape from Egypt and long trek to the Promised Land. Thus, the way is opened for exegetes to treat the Bible according to the mode of Plutarch. The sacred history must submit to a purification by reason, set critically against other historical sources. But in so doing, one can no longer treat it as sacred.[42]

In *Discourses on Livy*, Machiavelli attempted to construct a critical history, where his "great labor is the recovery of history (or better, the pagan wisdom about history) shorn of the Christian overlay and interpretation."[43] Implied in this work is Machiavelli's move away from religious truth to the question of political value. In keeping with the Latin Averroist tradition, Machiavelli viewed religion in terms of political expedience; it was a tool that could be helpful in exercising and maintaining control. In contrast to Averroës's hierarchy, where philosophers like him stood at the pinnacle,

---

38. Hahn and Wiker, *Politicizing the Bible*, 128.
39. Hahn and Wiker, *Politicizing the Bible*, 130.
40. Hahn and Wiker, *Politicizing the Bible*, 131.
41. Hahn and Wiker, *Politicizing the Bible*, 131.
42. Hahn and Wiker, *Politicizing the Bible*, 134–35.
43. Hahn and Wiker, *Politicizing the Bible*, 138.

Machiavelli's emphasis was on politics and the way in which good princes could use religion to control their people. Thus, Hahn and Wiker consider Machiavelli to be "one of the earliest, and certainly the most influential, sources of the hermeneutics of suspicion."[44] They explain quite well the way this will play out over time:

> The biblical text contains a largely hidden message that only the wise can see.... But once we are enlightened, then we, too, can interpret the text correctly.... To reason about Moses with Machiavelli means to offer an account of what really happened, appearances or reports in the text to the contrary.... The pattern set is one in which the philosophy, no matter how far removed it is from the assumptions of the biblical text, becomes the secret knowledge that allows the exegete to wield the exegetical threshing tool.... The task of the enlightened exegete, then, is to ferret out all the "real" passages—the ones that fit the philosophy—and reinterpret the rest, giving some *other* explanation for their appearance in the text.[45]

Machiavelli's influence would continue in the course of the history of biblical interpretation, not only through Spinoza, his avid reader, but also in the history of New Testament scholarship and the early quest for the historical Jesus with the figure of Hermann Samuel Reimarus (1694–1768), whose doctoral dissertation was on Machiavelli.

Two Kingdoms: The Protestant Reformation and the New Biblical Exegesis

Martin Luther (1483–1546) was not the only important figure within the Protestant Reformation, but he is of towering significance.[46] Luther cannot be adequately understood apart from his broader nominalist context. Luther famously confessed Ockham to be both "the greatest dialectician" and Luther's own "master," among whose followers Luther numbers himself and whose teachings he claims to "have absorbed completely."[47] Luther's separation of faith and reason, which paved the way for the de-Hellenization of

---

44. Hahn and Wiker, *Politicizing the Bible*, 144.
45. Hahn and Wiker, *Politicizing the Bible*, 145.
46. For what follows on Luther and the Protestant Reformation, see Hahn and Wiker, *Politicizing the Bible*, 147–219.
47. Hahn and Wiker, *Politicizing the Bible*, 148.

Scripture within modern biblical scholarship, was almost certainly influenced by Luther's nominalism, mediated to him by Gabriel Biel (1420–1495). Hahn and Wiker point out that: "Ironically, in setting reason free in its own domain, nominalism contributed to its secularization, therefore duplicating the quasi-Averroist framework found in Marsilius of Padua."[48]

The Reformation's political context provides the essential lens for understanding the Reformation itself as well as Luther's theology and exegetical arguments.[49] Reformation historians R. W. Scribner and C. Scott Dixon underscore that: "From the very beginning, the question of religious reform was so inextricably linked to political issues that it could never give rise to an unpolitical Reformation."[50] This is not only an important context within which to understand the Reformation in general but also Luther specifically, as Martin Brecht makes clear:

> From the very beginning, in Wittenberg, the monk Martin Luther was in a powerful political arena, even though at first he knew nothing about it. That he himself became a factor in this arena had religious and theological reasons. From the very moment when Luther appeared, speaking and acting independently, his involvement in a concrete political and social context also became inevitable.[51]

The primary political context was the burgeoning throne versus altar conflict, which is characteristically, albeit anachronistically, traced back to the medieval period. Key aspects of that narrative, however, are significant at this time. What is often mistaken as a church-state conflict in the medieval period is, as Andrew Jones has shown, the temporal and ecclesiastical authorities helping keep each other in check so as to further the business of the peace and the faith, a common goal they shared but in different ways.[52] These conflicts, however, eventually did become rival battles for authority. Financial interests were an important part of these conflicts, and as shared concerns for the business of the peace and the faith eroded and, eventually, Christendom was splintered into rival conceptions of Christian society, the

---

48. Hahn and Wiker, *Politicizing the Bible*, 149.

49. One of the few studies dealing with early modern contributions to historical biblical criticism that get the role of politics and the Reformation is Frampton, *Spinoza and the Rise of Historical Criticism*, especially 23–42.

50. Scribner and Dixon, *German Reformation*, 35.

51. Brecht, *Martin Luther*, 113.

52. See Jones, *Before Church and State*.

throne versus altar conflicts became just that: temporal and ecclesiastical rulers vying for authority.

In Luther's context, the history of money flowing out of what would become Germany to the Papal States is of prime importance. When Machiavelli was a Florentine diplomat, he had dealings with Maximilian I, the Holy Roman Emperor, who desired to rule the northern regions of the Papal States. At the same time, the Holy Roman Emperor was also in conflict with Frederick III (as well as the other German electors). Frederick III, the Elector of Saxony, would become Luther's protector, and this fact makes his role in the story more obvious than hidden. Frederick III resented papal taxation. He was upset with the fact that money which could have been for his own purposes and within his own kingdom was instead flowing out of the German realm to Rome. Frederick was in conflict with his own, noble-born Catholic bishops, and thus, he was a prime political candidate to serve as Luther's protector when the time came.

There is a way in which Luther's *Ninety-Five Theses* can be understood within the earlier context of the poverty debate and other prior reform movements. The *Ninety-Five Theses* actually fits rather well within the boundaries of Catholicism of that time.[53] Hahn and Wiker go so far as to assert that: "If Martin Luther's criticisms of the Church had remained as they appeared in his ninety-five theses . . . there would likely have been no Protestant Reformation (or, at least, not one associated with Luther)."[54] They are able to say this because, as they point out: "Luther's concern was originally with the *abuse* of indulgences,"[55] not with the doing away with indulgences or other Catholic teachings. Indeed, there are several places within the *Ninety-Five Theses* where Luther even writes favorably about indulgences (e.g., thesis 71).[56] Regarding the *Ninety-Five Theses*, Gary Anderson comments: "What emerges from this discussion is the significance of traditional acts of charity as opposed to the act of buying indulgences to assist in the refurbishing of St. Peter's. Luther's critique is not Church-dividing; he is at this point of his career a reformer within the bounds of Catholic thought."[57]

---

53. For the broader context here, see Moorman, *Indulgences*.
54. Hahn and Wiker, *Politicizing the Bible*, 158.
55. Hahn and Wiker, *Politicizing the Bible*, 159.
56. On this, see also Anderson, *Charity*, 185; Anderson, "Redeem Your Sins," 66–69, 68–69n71.
57. Anderson, "Redeem Your Sins," 69n71.

From the perspective of many in the region that would later become Germany, money that was part of the system of indulgences left the realm in large sums and went to the pope in Rome. Luther's call for reform regarding indulgences found an instant hearing among those who were already upset with the loss of revenue, especially among the German rulers. His reform on matters of indulgences fit nicely into the broader, nationalistic desires and the people's dissatisfaction with papal use of funds gained through indulgences that had a long history already. Hahn and Wiker observe that: "Unlike France and England, Germany had so far been unable to establish a kind of national church in which the monetary benefits remained largely within the realm."[58] Similarly, William Cavanaugh explains that:

> There is a direct relationship between the success of efforts to restrict supra-national Church authority and the failure of the Reformation within those realms. In other words, wherever concordats between the Papal See and temporal rulers had already limited the jurisdiction of the Church within national boundaries, there the princes saw no need to throw off the yoke of Catholicism, precisely because Catholicism had already been reduced, to a greater extent, to a suasive body under the heel of the secular power.[59]

Writing near the end of their chapter on Luther, Hahn and Wiker elaborate:

> Without the desire for a national church, without national resentment between Italy and Germany, without German envy of the "national" church of the French and the justified feeling that many Catholics were self-interested Romanists, without the protection of Romantic-messianic nationalists like [Ulrich von] Hutten, without the shield of the German princes, it is difficult to see how Lutheranism could have taken hold.[60]

The question of "method" for biblical interpretation—a method that prescinded from Catholic tradition—would only emerge after Luther argued for Scripture as prime authority, what would later become known as the Protestant doctrine of *sola Scriptura*. Luther constructed doctrine of two kingdoms, church and state, placing control of the temporal realm,

---

58. Hahn and Wiker, *Politicizing the Bible*, 160.

59. Cavanaugh, "Fire Strong Enough," 400–401. See also Cavanaugh, *Myth of Religious Violence*, especially chapter 3, "Creation Myth of the Wars of Religion," 123–80 (and regarding the discussion here, particularly 166–70), where he revisits the thesis of his "Fire Strong Enough," expanding it significantly.

60. Hahn and Wiker, *Politicizing the Bible*, 218.

including individual bodies, firmly in the hands of the state, in partial response to the numerous theological debates that erupted in the wake of his challenges to Catholic tradition as an authority. For Luther, the state would exercise rule over the temporal realm; an argument more along the lines of what Wycliffe had previously argued than what had been a normal part of the medieval discourse, as Andrew Jones described it. Luther's arguments concerning the "priesthood of all believers," sole authority in Scripture, and individual interpretation apart from tradition inspired the peasant's violent revolt, which led Luther to change his own position, arguing instead that biblical interpreters must first be trained adequately. Hahn and Wiker explain the upshot of Luther's proposition, hinting at the trajectory of these arguments:

> Luther wanted to keep the papacy from claiming sole power to determine the meaning of Scripture as justification for its worldly use of power. But in conferring the power to interpret Scripture on all the laity, he inadvertently gave to secular sovereigns the kind of power over Scripture advocated by Marsilius and German nationalist humanists like Hutten, and also empowered multiple theological revolutions from below without a *traditio* to constrain them.[61]

Luther's concept of salvation (justification) apart from works and by faith alone (*sola fide*) became the interpretive lens through which Luther read the rest of Scripture. He replaced the spiritual sense of typology with his own notion of "promise" and "fulfillment." Luther aligned himself with Ockham's own critique of the spiritual sense, both grounded in their frustrations with how the spiritual sense had been used to understand the "two swords" in defense of papal authority. Luther thus effected a transformation in biblical hermeneutics. No longer was Scripture's home primarily to be at the sacred liturgy, it was now primarily a text for individual Christians. Moreover, as opposed to recourse to the two senses of Scripture, the literal and spiritual, Luther replaced these with a series of dichotomies: spirit versus letter; gospel versus law; New Testament versus Old Testament; etc. Hahn and Wiker point out that: "In this dialectical hermeneutic, the Old Testament serves a largely negative function as law, rather than serving as the priestly, sacrificial foundation to be fulfilled in the New Testament."[62]

---

61. Hahn and Wiker, *Politicizing the Bible*, 170.

62. Hahn and Wiker, *Politicizing the Bible*, 175. Even though he focused on the literal sense, it is not quite accurate to see Luther's fundamental significance exegetically as emphasizing the literal sense, as Hahn and Wiker caution: "It is misleading ... to assume

This will play out in significant ways in later historical criticism and into the nineteenth and twentieth centuries.

In keeping with his new development of two kingdoms, Luther encouraged the state in its enforcement of "orthodoxy." This was part of Luther's response to the peasants' revolt and the eruption of mutually exclusive biblical interpretations and theologies, all allegedly grounded in Scripture, in the wake of his clarion calls for reform and his severing of ties with tradition, coupled with the claim that each (e.g., the peasants) were faithful followers of him. He began to realize, in Hahn and Wiker's words, that "the Bible in the hands of the masses is a dangerous thing."[63] Like Wycliffe before him, Luther argued for state control of the temporal realm, including church offices, which he understood to be exterior, temporal, or secular. Luther thereby "contributed to the creation of an entirely secular political order."[64] Hahn and Wiker explain the significance of Luther's two kingdoms doctrine:

> Since Luther viewed political power as an ordained external force to keep sinners under control (rather than, as with Aristotle and St. Thomas [Aquinas], a positive order that helps perfect natural potentialities), his tendency (with Thomas Hobbes after him) was to view political order, no matter how harsh, as vindicated solely because any political order was better than the complete anarchy (the chaos of Satan) that would inevitably break loose without it.[65]

The German nobility welcomed Luther's theology since it provided a theoretical justification for their opposition to Rome, as well as to the revolting peasants, who Luther encouraged them to fight ruthlessly. Luther urged them to "smash, strangle, and stab, secretly or openly,"[66] the peasants involved in the rebellion, "as a matter of Christian duty."[67] Again, as Hahn and Wiker make clear: "Luther's doctrines did provide a way for German princes to break from Rome and remain entirely in charge of the religion

---

that the importance of Luther as an exegete is his focus on the literal account of Scripture; rather, his importance consists in substituting the dialectical mode of exegesis for the traditional fourfold meaning of Scripture" (Hahn and Wiker, *Politicizing the Bible*, 177).

63. Hahn and Wiker, *Politicizing the Bible*, 194.
64. Hahn and Wiker, *Politicizing the Bible*, 203.
65. Hahn and Wiker, *Politicizing the Bible*, 204.
66. Marius, *Martin Luther*, 431, as quoted in Hahn and Wiker, *Politicizing the Bible*, 210.
67. Hahn and Wiker, *Politicizing the Bible*, 210.

within their own peaceful realm, equally protected from the dangers of the likes of Karlstadt, Müntzers, and the Zwickau prophets."[68]

To be fair, these princes who supported Luther may have had sincere doctrinal motives, but we certainly cannot know this since such interior motives are private. Here, it is worth revisiting the lengthy quotation from Reformation historians R. W. Scribner and C. Scott Dixon[69] on the often neglected political aspects of the Protestant Reformation's success in Germany:

> After a brief period of mass enthusiasm, it [support for the Reformation] retreated to being a minority phenomenon. At a crude estimate, during the first generation of the Reformation, up to mid-century, and perhaps even during the second, probably no more than 10 percent of the German population ever showed an active and lasting enthusiasm for reformed ideas. Where massive numbers were "won" after 1526, to what became the new church, it occurred involuntarily, through a prince deciding that his territory should adopt the new faith. When we speak of the extensive hold "Protestantism" had on Germany by the second half of the sixteenth century... this was because there were large numbers of "involuntary Protestants" created by the princes' confessional choices.[70]

Turning to biblical interpretation and Luther's significant role within the early history of modern biblical criticism, we can point to his development of a "canon within the canon" as having a lengthy influence, up to our present day. Luther's core canon—for him, the true gospel—only involved a few biblical books, all from the New Testament: Romans, Galatians, Ephesians, 1 Peter, and the Gospel of John. To be clear, these were not the only books Luther considered divinely inspired or included in his canon; rather, they were the ones he thought were perhaps most inspired. They were the ones containing what he thought was the true gospel message, in light of which all the other inspired books of Scripture must be read.

As we move forward in time within the history of modern biblical scholarship, we find biblical scholars moving beyond Luther's searching of the biblical canon to the scholarly quest for authentic portions of specific biblical books. Whereas Luther thought the questions of the canon

68. Hahn and Wiker, *Politicizing the Bible*, 210.

69. This crucial quotation also appears in Morrow, *Three Skeptics and the Bible*, 26–27.

70. Scribner and Dixon, *German Reformation*, 34. Something similar can be said for the English Reformation, as we shall see shortly. See Duffy, *Stripping of the Altars*.

entailed which books belonged in Scripture and which ones were most inspired or of primary importance, later biblical scholars would question the individual texts themselves, arguing for the evidence of later additions and corruptions in the text. They would thus sift the texts for an authentic, historical core in order to remove the inauthentic corruptions. In light of this and Luther's overall exegetical project, Hahn and Wiker conclude: "Despite Luther's intentions, playing the authority of the princes against the papacy meant inadvertently giving the authority over interpretation to the secular powers."[71]

"Stripping the Altars"[72]: The English Reformation

King Henry VIII (1491-1547, reigned 1509-1547) is an important and yet almost always overlooked figure within the history of modern biblical criticism.[73] His importance rests both in how his reign built upon the history that came before, which we have already covered—from Marsilius of Padua and Wycliffe to Machiavelli and Luther—but also in how the English Reformation he initiated prepared the ground for English Deistic biblical exegesis. In the eighteenth century, such English Deistic biblical interpretation would transplant to Germany and contribute significantly to Enlightenment biblical criticism. As Hahn and Wiker correctly point out: "England becomes the filter through which earlier developments are handed on to the Enlightenment."[74]

In order to understand King Henry VIII's significance here, it is important to view him within his immediate context, which must include the issue of the king's "Great Matter," involving his marriage to Anne Boleyn. Of course Henry's "Great Matter" was not what led to the English Reformation, but it was when the English Reformation began. In Hahn and Wiker's words, Henry's "Great Matter" became "the occasion" for the English Reformation.[75] The fact that his desire to divorce his wife and marry Anne Boleyn ended up involving theologians and biblical interpreters from across Europe helps us catch a glimpse of its significance beyond merely

---

71. Hahn and Wiker, *Politicizing the Bible*, 217.

72. Subheading taken from Duffy, *Stripping the Altars*.

73. For what follows on King Henry VIII and the English Reformation, see Hahn and Wiker, *Politicizing the Bible*, 221-55.

74. Hahn and Wiker, *Politicizing the Bible*, 221-22.

75. Hahn and Wiker, *Politicizing the Bible*, 223.

biographical details. The debate that erupted involved questions of biblical interpretation at universities in numerous nations, including both Catholic and Protestant interpreters.

Ironically, Henry VIII, as Catholic monarch of England, defended the Catholic Church's teaching against divorce in the wake of Protestant challenges to Church teaching. He argued that the concept that divorce was inadmissible was one of the distinctive Christian teachings that dignified Christian marriage from other forms of marriage in other traditions. When Luther, Philip Melanchthon (1497–1560), and Martin Bucer (1491–1551) argued that divorce and bigamy (if not polygamy) might be acceptable in Christian marriage under certain circumstances, King Henry VIII came to the rescue, defending the Catholic teaching on marriage against these Protestant Reformers. The occasion for Protestant discussion on this topic was Philip of Hesse's (1504–1567) attempt at taking a second wife. Philip of Hesse had championed the Protestant cause and thus leading figures like Luther wrote of marriage in a non-sacramental way, which aided their case that divorce and bigamy might be permissible. King Henry would have none of that. He wrote a response defending marriage as an inviolable sacrament, and thus divorce, bigamy, polygamy, etc., were impermissible, as had always been the case within Christianity.

Eventually, with the support of a number of his court theologians, Henry began to argue, based on the Bible, that his marriage to Catherine of Aragon was invalid. He used Leviticus 18:16, which prohibited committing adultery with the wife of one's brother, as support for his claim. The fact that his brother was dead and that he had been given permission to marry Catherine did not appear to trouble Henry so much. More concerning for him was the punishment of Leviticus 20:21, which was attached to breaking Leviticus 18:16—namely, that they will be childless. Henry interpreted this to be the reason behind their inability to have a son that could serve as an heir. That is, Henry claimed God was punishing him with no male heir because he was married to Catherine who had been his brother's wife.

This conflict became the brunt of controversy across Europe, involving theologians and biblical interpreters across nations. Theologians wrote to the king, explaining why he should marry Anne or why he should instead remain faithful to Catherine. Soon Anne became pregnant, but the two remained unwed. Henry took drastic action and married her privately. It was only after their private marriage that Henry's marriage to Catherine was annulled. The Archbishop of Canterbury, whom Henry appointed, formally annulled Henry's marriage, and thus the split with Rome was concrete; it was not the pope who granted the annulment but rather the state of England, headed by England's King. In Hahn and Wiker's words, this is when "the Church *in* England" became "the Church *of* England."[76]

Hahn and Wiker have uncovered some evidence that indicates there may have been Machiavellian and Marsilian influence on Henry's reform in England, particularly through the policies enacted and the policy-makers behind the scenes. Some of Henry's confidants and some of those defending his policies throughout England, e.g., Richard Morison (1513–1556) and Thomas Starkey (1495–1538), used the works of both Machiavelli and Marsilius (mainly his *Defensor Pacis*). Marsilius's work—read through the later context of sixteenth-century England and not through Marsilius's own late medieval context—became a sort of blueprint for Henrician reform policies in England. Thomas Cromwell (1485–1540) may have been influenced by Machiavelli's works himself, but he was certainly the figure responsible for the publication of *Defensor Pacis* in English translation. Under Henry VIII's reforms, Marsilius's program, which may have fit within its medieval context, became a violent, secularizing force in sixteenth-century England, subordinating church to state, where no such clear distinctions had existed prior.

We thus find influences on the Henrician regime stemming from Marsilius of Padua, Wycliffe, and Machiavelli. All of these figures laid important groundwork for what would occur in the Reformation of England, which paved the way for the Deistic exegesis that would eventually find a home in eighteenth-century Germany. As Hahn and Wiker observe, "We have then, in Henry, both in theory and fact, a Marsilian ruler, not an emperor but a national king, a man in both person and policy that brought the pages of the *Defensor Pacis* to life in England. . . . Henry provided an example of Machiavellianism as vivid as Pope Alexander VI."[77] In the next chapter, we will see how the work of the seventeenth century built upon this prior history. We will focus on and expand upon the key figures already discussed in *Three Skeptics and the Bible*: Isaac La Peyrère (1596–1676), Thomas Hobbes (1588–1679), and Baruch Spinoza (1632–1677).

---

76. Hahn and Wiker, *Politicizing the Bible*, 236.
77. Hahn and Wiker, *Politicizing the Bible*, 254.

2

Corrosive History

Pioneer Biblical Critics

ISAAC LA PEYRÈRE (1596–1676), Thomas Hobbes (1588–1679), and Baruch Spinoza (1632–1677) are increasingly identified with the foundation of modern historical biblical criticism in the seventeenth century. Because of this, I chose to focus on these figures in my previous book, *Three Skeptics and the Bible*.[1] Although these figures have late medieval and early modern precursors who aided the development of modern biblical criticism, as we saw in the previous chapter, their work contrasts significantly with prior exegesis, especially regarding the distance they placed between themselves and the biblical texts. They approached the Scripture from a modern position of skepticism, much more so than had most of their predecessors, with the exception of Machiavelli. Moreover, many of the exegetical moves these figures made in the middle part and in the second half of the seventeenth century were developed further in the eighteenth and nineteenth centuries, finally solidifying an exegesis recognizable as the historical criticism of the Bible still found in contemporary university settings.

The work of these three was foundational and even indispensable to the Enlightenment project. This is especially the case with Spinoza, who created the methodological blueprint that later biblical critics would follow.[2] When one examines the social and political background of these three biblical interpreters, it is apparent that they utilized the then-newly-developing, modern discipline of history as an acid to dissolve traditional theological interpretations of Scripture. They then redeployed what remained of the Bible for their own political projects. These projects were inextricably bound up with the theo-political goals of the newly formed modern European states

---

1. Morrow, *Three Skeptics and the Bible*.
2. See Morrow, "Spinoza and the Theo-Political Implications," 374–87.

that had emerged after the violent sixteenth and seventeenth century "wars of religion." The foundations these three figures laid would be built upon by Enlightenment exegetes from their academic chairs in eighteenth and nineteenth-century German universities. Those who continue to inherit this form of biblical interpretation generally accept the fundamental assumptions of this exegesis without appreciating that these assumptions originate in the political exegesis of the seventeenth century.

It was for these important reasons that I chose to focus on these figures in *Three Skeptics and the Bible*, but they merit revisiting here. I have done additional work since then, uncovering further material which strengthens the claims found in *Three Skeptics and the Bible*. Thus, in this chapter, I begin walking forward chronologically with the life and work of La Peyrère. La Peyrère presents a method for reading Scripture which he had created ad hoc in order to justify his peculiar political exegesis. In itself, this would not be very important for a study such as the one I am undertaking; it could be just a simple case of proof-texting to prove a point. La Peyrère's significance, however, lies in the fact that his work was followed by other key seventeenth-century figures. Moreover, his work continues to garner responses, with scholars having built upon his foundations in an ever more systematic fashion for over two centuries, including the present. Indeed, the great Old Testament scholar Julius Wellhausen (1844–1918), often hailed as the father of the Documentary Hypothesis, traced the origin of such Pentateuch criticism by name to La Peyrère.[3]

The next figure to consider is Hobbes, the famous English political philosopher and one of the architects of modern liberal politics. It is not because Hobbes concocted an ad hoc method of biblical interpretation to suit his political ends—like La Peyrère—that Hobbes is significant; rather, it is because his exegetical work was followed and reacted against by so many of those exegetes who came after, as also happened with La Peyrère.

After Hobbes, I examine the erstwhile Jewish philosopher Spinoza. It is with Spinoza that we find, for the first time, a well-thought out and precisely constructed hermeneutic for biblical exegesis, not along theological grounds, but ostensibly following a rigorous scientific method. Spinoza, who was a major focus of both *Three Skeptics and the Bible*[4] and my *Theology, Politics, and Exegesis*,[5] emerges as one of the most significant—if not

---

3. Wellhausen, *Prolegomena*, 6.
4. Morrow, *Three Skeptics and the Bible*, 104–38, 148–51.
5. Morrow, *Theology, Politics, and Exegesis*, 16–34.

the most significant—precursors to modern biblical scholars. Thus, he certainly merits revisiting here.

Each of these three figures approaches the biblical text and traditional theological exegesis from a position of skepticism. Not surprisingly, their exegesis is ill-suited for theological endeavors, especially the pursuit of holiness. Instead, such historical methods enable one to bypass traditional theological authorities, which, once secularized, play a role little stronger than mere private opinion; the Church becomes merely suasive, without any disciplinary authority. The practical pastoral results are ensured from the get go: such exegesis is intended to produce good civil servants who give their absolute obedience to the state. The intent, especially clear in Hobbes and Spinoza, is to quell violent conflict they identify as originating in theological conviction, but, conveniently, such exegesis leaves no room for martyrdom either; rather, it sanctions unlimited, unapologetic state violence against anyone the state determines to be a threat to absolute sovereignty. The targets are those such as St. John Fisher and St. Thomas More from the previous century, as well as any future St. John Fishers and St. Thomas Mores.[6]

A Heap of Copies Carelessly Made: Isaac La Peyrère

Isaac La Peyrère was born in Bordeaux, France, in about 1596.[7] The son of an affluent Huguenot family, La Peyrère took up employment in the service of the Prince of Condé in 1640 (first, Henry II de Bourbon, and then, after 1646, his immediate successor, Louis II de Bourbon). La Peyrère officially served as Condé's personal secretary, but his duties involved numerous diplomatic missions, and La Peyrère's work was inextricably bound up with Condé's varied political exploits. La Peyrère is important for our discussion because of a book he wrote at the urging of Descartes's patroness, Queen Christina of Sweden. La Peyrère entitled the book, *Prae-Adamitae* (*Pre-Adamites*).[8] In published form, it was bound with his more

---

6. For the contrast with St. Thomas More's exegesis, see Morrow, *Theology, Politics, and Exegesis*, 35–51; and Morrow, "Thomas More," 365–73.

7. For biographical information about La Peyrère, see Pietsch, *Isaac La Peyrère*, 1–3, 25–33, 44–46, 71–73, 85–86, 125–33, 162–67; Morrow, *Three Skeptics and the Bible*, 54–84; Nellen, "Growing Tension," 817–23; Popkin, *Isaac La Peyrère*, 5–25.

8. La Peyrère, *Prae-Adamitae*. The work was translated into English as La Peyrère, *Men before Adam*. All English translations in this essay will be taken from this version.

complete treatment, *Systema Theologicum* (*Theological System*), where he elaborated on his new biblical hermeneutic.⁹ Both of these works were initially published anonymously in 1655. *Prae-Adamitae*, however, circulated in unpublished form over a decade earlier. In fact, published refutations of *Prae-Adamitae* began to appear throughout Europe long before *Prae-Adamitae* was actually published.

In *Prae-Adamitae* and *Systema Theologicum*, La Peyrère chiseled away at Sacred Scripture with the corrosive acids of his skeptical hermeneutic under the guise of historical enquiry. Although La Peyrère is often mentioned as a pioneer of modern historical biblical criticism and a central transitional figure, he never pretended to formulate a consistent historical method as such; rather, he set out to prove the need for reading the Bible anew through the lenses of his political eschatology.¹⁰ Moreover, La Peyrère had many important precursors (e.g., Joseph Scaliger), thus, he was neither the first to criticize the biblical text nor the first to utilize extrabiblical historical works from other cultures in order to interpret the Bible.¹¹

La Peyrère clearly built upon the work of others, but he also wrested the Bible from the hands of theologians and philologists alike in order to utilize the Good Book for another purpose.¹² That purpose was nothing other than the transformation of Scripture into a political weapon. That the Bible had been used for political ends in the past cannot be doubted, but La Peyrère wished to appropriate the Sacred Page for his own secular end, or, rather, in support of the political machinations of his employer, Condé. As Richard Popkin, the scholar who has written the most about La Peyrère, underscored over a decade ago: "What was being proposed in La Peyrère's first work was not a pipe dream but a program of political action."¹³ When he set down his quill, what emerged was a Bible that was only decipherable

---

9. La Peyrère, *Systema Theologicum*. The was likewise translated into English as La Peyrère, *Theological Systeme*.

10. On his important place in this history, see the references to La Peyrère in Barthélemy, *Studies in the Text*, 52–53; Titzmann, "Herausforderungen der biblischen Hermeneutik," 147–49, 153–54; Kugel, *How to Read the Bible*, 696n39; Goshen-Gottstein, "Textual Criticism," 376; Wellhausen, *Prolegomena*, 6.

11. On Scaliger, see especially Grafton, *Joseph Scaliger I–II*.

12. La Peyrère explicitly cited Scaliger in *Systema Theologicum*, 3.7.180, 3.8.181, 4.9.232, 4.13.244. That La Peyrère did not use Scaliger accurately has been made clear by Quennehen, "Lapeyrère," 243–55.

13. Popkin, "Millenarianism and Nationalism," 78. Popkin published around twenty books, articles, and essays dealing in some way with La Peyrère's work.

through La Peyrère's French nationalistic messianic vision; a Bible waiting to be redeployed as a powerful tool of statecraft.[14]

La Peyrère's approach is complex, but it can be simplified by identifying a general two-pronged procedure he used in constructing an informal biblical hermeneutic by deconstructing Scripture. First, he hoped to demonstrate that the traditional way of reading Scripture's account of creation in Genesis was wrong. Secondly, he sought to emphasize the inadequacy of traditional attitudes toward Scripture and exegesis by exposing a multitude of difficulties (concerning authorship, text, style, and narrative) in light of the actual facts concerning the Bible.

The first thing La Peyrère attempts to show his readers is how the broad history of the tradition of interpreting creation in Genesis has gotten it all wrong. This was quite a feat, considering how incredibly broad Jewish and Christian interpretations of Genesis 1–2 had been over the previous well-over millennium-and-a-half by the time of La Peyrère's writing. La Peyrère based his arguments in part on his idiosyncratic reading of Romans 5:12–14. His overarching contention was that, whereas Genesis 1–2 had traditionally been read as an account of the creation of all of humanity, descendants of Adam and Eve, this was a misinterpretation. Instead, La Peyrère suggests, Adam and Eve are the first parents of the Jewish people exclusively. On La Peyrère's reading, Genesis 1 depicts the creation of pre-Adamites, the "men before Adam"—that is, Gentiles.[15] La Peyrère was not the first to have proposed an interpretation like this one (which already existed in the Muslim world), but his was the most influential, pre-Adamite hypothesis in history, and it perdured into the nineteenth century, where it was used in justifications of slavery.[16]

La Peyrère's next move was to discredit the biblical text by demonstrating that the traditional attributions of authorship of the various books of the Old Testament were almost certainly false, followed by his attempt to point out textual, stylistic, and narrative difficulties within the Scripture. La Peyrère arguably went further in discrediting the biblical account than any prior

---

14. That this is the case has been shown in Morrow, *Three Skeptics and the Bible*, 54–84; Popkin, "Millenarianism and Nationalism," 74–84.

15. La Peyrère, *Prae-Adamitae*, 1–3, 7–8, 10.5–12, 27–28, 19.7, 9–11, 20, 45–46, 26.21–25, 58; La Peyrère, *Systema Theologicum*, 61, 1.1.65–68, 2.10.137–141; Morrow, *Three Skeptics and the Bible*, 54–84; van Asselt, "Adam en Eva," 104–6; Starobinski-Safran, "Raison et conflits," 100.

16. Subrahmanyam, "Intertwined Histories," 143–44; Almond, *Adam & Eve*, 164–66; Haarmann, "In Quest of the Spectacular," 65; and Popkin, "Pre-Adamite Theory," 50–69.

intellectual within the Christian tradition up until that time. The brunt of his attack was against the Mosaic authorship of the Pentateuch.[17] Attacks on the Mosaic authorship of the Pentateuch were not completely new by any stretch of the imagination, as is evidenced by their important place in Muslim, Roman, and Gnostic polemics against Judaism and Christianity.[18] What was new was the force with which La Peyrère used these criticisms to disembowel Scripture—and he did so from within the Christian tradition.

His arguments against the Mosaic authorship of the Pentateuch can be summed up as follows: (1) Deuteronomy 1:1 mentions the "Transjordan," implying that the author is already in the Promised Land; (2) Deuteronomy 34 mentions the death of Moses; (3) Deuteronomy 3:11 references a new location for "iron bed," which implies that it was moved somewhere else by the time the author wrote those words; (4) the recurring phrase in Deuteronomy "unto this day," implying that the "this day" of the author is later than the recounted events; (5) the phrase "as Israel did" in Deuteronomy 2:12 appears anachronistic; and (6) the reference to the document, "book of wars of the Lord," in Numbers 21:14.[19]

La Peyrère proceeded to other difficulties he detected in the Old Testament narratives. In this category, he included a host of details he simply found incredible and which he expects others to reject as foolish in turn, e.g., when Genesis 20 depicts the king Abimelech lusting after Abraham's wife Sarah. La Peyrère asserts: "It is not likely that the king would lust after Sarah, who was an old woman . . . and who was not capable of pleasure."[20] He penned the line which became (in)famous in the seventeenth century, that the Pentateuch was "neither the original nor a copy of the original but was a copy from a copy."[21] He thus concluded with an intentionally

---

17. On La Peyrère's critique of this traditional notion, see especially Morrow, *Three Skeptics and the Bible*, 54–84; Bernier, *La critique du Pentateuque*, 25, 27, 32, 39, 76, 121, 136–45, 157–58, 190, 222–23, 242–45, 254–55; Gibert, *L'invention critique*, 86–88, 112–13, 169, 207; Jorink, "Horrible and Blasphemous," 429; Popkin, *Third Force*, 16–18, 32–34, 37, 159, 352, 355.

18. On this history, see chapter 4 in this volume; Morrow, *Three Skeptics and the Bible*, 10–84; Bernier, *La critique du Pentateuque*; Gibert, *L'invention critique*, 84–93, 110–16, 166–95, 214–19; Homan, "How Moses Gained," 111–32; Malcolm, "*Leviathan*, the Pentateuch," 241–64; Gibert, *L'invention de l'exégèse*; Malcolm, *Aspects of Hobbes*, 383–431; Freedman, "Father of Modern Biblical Scholarship," 31–38; Rif'at, "Ibn Ḥazm on Jews," 220–94.

19. See La Peyrère, *Systema Theologicum*, 4.1.198–200.

20. La Peyrère, *Systema Theologicum*, 4.1.201 (English translation, slightly modified).

21. La Peyrère, *Systema Theologicum*, 4.1.199 (English translation, slightly modified).

dismissive remark: "No one need wonder after this, that one reads so many things which are confused and out of order, obscure, deficient, many things omitted and misplaced; since they shall understand that they [the Scriptures] are a heap of copies confusedly taken."[22]

Although he was not the first, it is significant that La Peyrère made use of material from other regions of the world (China, the Americas, Africa, northern Europe, etc.) in reconstructing his history of the Bible and of humanity.[23] All of these exegetical moves and methodological considerations served one purpose in La Peyrère's writings—namely, they supported his eschatological messianic vision, which he believed was to be fulfilled in his age. La Peyrère argued that there were two Messiahs: one for Christians, the second for Jews. The Jewish Messiah was to return and rule the world alongside his steward, the King of France.[24] What has since become clear is that La Peyrère's nationalistic, messianic vision was a theoretical bolster to the political ambitions of his employer Condé. La Peyrère appears to have been in the middle of an evolving plot to oust King Louis XIV from the throne and place Condé in his stead, as Protestant King of France. Queen Christina of Sweden and Oliver Cromwell were the other players in this drama. The plan failed, but La Peyrère's entire biblical exegetical project was a continuation of politics by other means. His biblical exegesis, which introduced a skeptical methodology, was aimed at political revolution.[25]

---

22. La Peyrère, *Systema Theologicum*, 4.1.201 (English translation, modified).

23. Morrow, *Three Skeptics and the Bible*, 54–84; Livingstone, "Cultural Politics," 207; Gabriel, "Periegesis and Skepticism," 159–70; Livingstone, *Adam's Ancestors*, 35, 44, 48–49; Benítez, "La posterité," 183–202.

24. La Peyrère, *Du Rappel des Juifs*; La Peyrère, "Synagogis Iudaeorum Universis, Quotuot sunt per totum Terrarum orbem sparsae," which was appended to *Prae-Adamitae*; Pietsch, *Isaac La Peyrère*, 107–39, 154–84; Morrow, *Three Skeptics and the Bible*, 54–84; Parente, "Isaac de La Peyrère," 169–86; Starobinski-Safran, "Raison et conflits," 97–98, 101–3; Popkin, "Millenarianism and Nationalism," 74–84; Haran, *Le lys et le globe*, 173–76; Parente, "Isaac de La Peyrère e Richard Simon," 171–78; Popkin, *Isaac La Peyrère*, 3, 8, 44, 50, 52–54, 58–59, 66.

25. Pietsch, *Isaac La Peyrère*, 127–40, 208–20; Morrow, *Three Skeptics and the Bible*, 54–84; Quennehen, "L'auteur des Préadamites," 349, 360, 365–66; Popkin, "Millenarianism and Nationalism," 78, 80, 82; Popkin, "First Published," 6–12; Popkin, "Jewish-Christian Relations," 165, 168; Åkerman, *Queen Christina*, 11, 200, 202–4, 213–15, 219; Popkin, *Isaac La Peyrère*, 3, 8–9, 12, 40, 58–60.

PRETENSIONS OF OBJECTIVITY

Of the Kingdome of Darknesse: Thomas Hobbes

Thomas Hobbes was born in England in 1588.[26] His life was bound up with the political circles in which he travelled, political circles that changed over time.[27] Hobbes, who was classically trained in Greek and Latin in the humanist tradition, was employed for the elite Cavendish family (serving as tutor for William Cavendish, Earl of Newcastle), and through this relationship, he was enabled to become a voting member of the Virginia Company.[28] Hobbes also served as the secretary to Francis Bacon.[29]

Unlike La Peyrère, Hobbes's emphasized the proper use of "reason" in biblical interpretation, and his conception of reason was grounded in what Blaise Pascal would call, *l'esprit géométrique* (the spirit of geometry)—that mathematics is the foundation of all reason and is the paradigmatic form of reason.[30] This perspective of Hobbes is made clear in his words: "Geometry . . . is the only Science that it has pleased God thus far to bestow on mankind."[31] For Hobbes, such reason was completely separate from faith.[32] The Thirty Years' War and the English Civil War serve as one of the most important contexts for understanding Hobbes's work on history and

---

26. For biographical information on Hobbes, see Morrow, *Three Skeptics and the Bible*, 85–103; Hahn and Wiker, *Politicizing the Bible*, 285–338; Reventlow, *History of Biblical Interpretation*, 4:32–51; Gillespie, *Theological Origins*, 206–54; Malcolm, *Reason of State*, 1–15; Martinich, *Hobbes*; Malcolm, "Summary Biography," 13–44; Reventlow, *Authority of the Bible*, 194–222.

27. Malcolm ed., *Leviathan*, 1:1–35, 1:61–87; Malcolm, *Reason of State*, 74–91.

28. Morrow, *Three Skeptics and the Bible*, 85–103; Hahn and Wiker, *Politicizing the Bible*, 289–90; Malcolm ed., *Leviathan*, 1:11–12, 1:166–68; Reventlow, *History of Biblical Interpretation* 4, 32–33; Gillespie, *Theological Origins*, 213–17; Malcolm, *Reason of State*, 1–15, 22–24, 75–76, 82; Schuhmann, "Hobbes's Concept," 3–4; Tuck, "Hobbes and Tacitus," 100; Skinner, *Reason and Rhetoric*, 19–40, 215–49; Malcolm, "Hobbes, Sandys," 297–321.

29. Morrow, *Three Skeptics and the Bible*, 85–103; Hahn and Wiker, *Politicizing the Bible*, 289; Gillespie, *Theological Origins of Modernity*, 215; Malcolm, *Reason of State*, 7–8; Bunce, "Thomas Hobbes's Relationship," 41–83; Rogers, "Hobbes, History," 77; Tuck, "Hobbes and Tacitus," 100, 108; Martinich, *Hobbes*, 43, 65–66.

30. Morrow, *Three Skeptics and the Bible*, 85–103, 139–48; Hahn and Wiker, *Politicizing the Bible*, 285, 290, 304.

31 All citations from Hobbes's *Leviathan* are taken from Malcolm ed., *Leviathan* 2–3. I have slightly modernized the English where Malcolm has left it in Hobbes's original. This quotation is taken from I.4 in *Leviathan*, 2:56. Hobbes's Latin translation simply reads, "Geometry, which alone is accurate Science" (Malcolm ed., *Leviathan*, 2:57).

32. Barnouw, "Separation of Reason," 607, 609–10, and 616–19.

specifically biblical interpretation.³³ In light of these conflicts, in which he envisioned religious factions to have played a central part, Hobbes brought a new biblical hermeneutic to bear that would yield a new exegesis, one which served the state and thus would serve as a herald of peace.³⁴

For Hobbes, the state sovereign had the authority to interpret Scripture or to appoint official interpreters.³⁵ In Hobbes's words, "It is the Civil Sovereign that is to appoint judges and interpreters of the canonical Scriptures, for it is he that makes them laws."³⁶ And earlier, "Whosoever in a Christian commonwealth holds the place of Moses [i.e., the sovereign] is the sole messenger of God and interpreter of his commandments. . . . No man ought in the interpretation of Scripture to proceed further than the bounds which are set by their several sovereigns."³⁷

In his work, especially *Leviathan*, Hobbes domesticated biblical miracles, either naturalizing them or else interpreting them as a means of bolstering support for earthly mediators (state rulers like Moses).³⁸ He thus naturalized most supernatural phenomena in Scripture throughout *Leviathan*.³⁹ An important reason for this was to support Hobbes's totalizing

---

33. Morrow, *Three Skeptics and the Bible*, 85–103 and 139–48; Hahn and Wiker, *Politicizing the Bible*, 286, 291–92, 300, 315, and 337–38; Levering, *Participatory Biblical Exegesis*, 108; Gillespie, *Theological Origins*, 238, 243–44, and 246; and Levenson, *Hebrew Bible*, 117.

34. Morrow, *Three Skeptics and the Bible*, 85–103 and 139–48; and Hahn and Wiker, *Politicizing the Bible*, 292 and 300.

35. Morrow, *Three Skeptics and the Bible*, 10–53, 85–103, and 139–48; Hahn and Wiker, *Politicizing the Bible*, 300, 313, 315, and 318; Nelson, *Hebrew Republic*, 125; Levering, *Participatory Biblical Exegesis*, 108; Gillespie, *Theological Origins*, 248; and Reventlow, *Authority of the Bible*, 213. We can see, for example, that when Hobbes makes an interpretation, he adds the caveat, "with submission nevertheless both in this, and in all questions, whereof the determination depends on the Scriptures, to the interpretation of the Bible authorized by the Commonwealth, whose subject I am." *Leviathan* III.38 in *Leviathan* 3, 698 and 700. Indeed, he makes similar comments about the very authority of Scripture as well, that Scripture's authority and canon derives from the sovereign's recognition and acceptance of it, not from some independent divine inspiration. Karl Schuhmann observes, "Hobbes correspondingly feels authorized to put Scripture and 'other history' sometimes on equal footing. . . . It is rather the legitimacy of this claim which gives canonical writings a unique position. And this legitimacy resides in the fact that they were recognized as authoritative by the Church, which (in the last instance) is to say, the sovereign" (Schuhmann, "Hobbes's Concept," 17).

36. *Leviathan* III.42 in Malcolm ed., *Leviathan*, 3:866.

37. *Leviathan* III.40 in Malcolm ed., *Leviathan*, 3:744.

38. Hahn and Wiker, *Politicizing the Bible*, 314–15.

39. Morrow, *Three Skeptics and the Bible*, 85–103; Hahn and Wiker, *Politicizing the*

claims about the state sovereign. If there can be a fear that is greater than death—say, the afterlife—then there can be a foreign religious authority (like the Pope in Rome) who wields a power beyond the grasp of the state sovereign. Thus, for Hobbes, there was no fate worse than death, no reason for martyrdom, no heaven or hell apart from the terrestrial good graces of or punishment by the ruling state sovereign.

As one means of bolstering his exegetical argument, Hobbes, like La Peyrère, attacked traditional notions of biblical authorship and authority. Notably, as with La Peyrère, Hobbes denied the substantial Mosaic authorship of the Pentateuch.[40] It should be made clear that Hobbes did not deny the Mosaic authorship of every passage of the Pentateuch (although he did deny Moses's authorship of the bulk of it) and that he also applied similar methods to the question of sources for the rest of the Bible (both the Old and New Testament). He cast doubt on traditional attributions of authorship in order to underscore the authority of the (official) exegete, which, for Hobbes, was the state ruler or state-appointed interpreter. He drove "exegetical wedges between the biblical characters (e.g., Moses) and the later compilers and editors . . . *for the sake of* the political sovereign's right to declare both canon and interpretation."[41] As Noel Malcolm explains: "What he objected to, however, was the idea that any text could have operated, through the centuries after Moses, as an independent locus of authority—independent, that is, of the political rulers of the day."[42] The point is that the Scriptures do not get authority from some form of divine inspiration of the text or the authors but rather from the political rulers who grant the Scriptures their authority.

It is in this context that Hobbes's attacked typology.[43] Typology moves forward toward fulfillment. This movement tends to be mystagogical in that

---

Bible, 324–34.

40. Morrow, *Three Skeptics and the Bible*, 10–53, 85–103; Hahn and Wiker, *Politicizing the Bible*, 321–22; Barthélemy, *Studies in the Text*, 52; Bernier, *La critique du Pentateuque*, 25, 48, 127–32, 139, 143–45; Reventlow, *History of Biblical Interpretation*, 4:44–45; Martinich, "Bible and Protestantism," 377–78; Kugel, *How to Read the Bible*, 29–31; Malcolm, "*Leviathan*," 241; Lessay, "Hobbes and Sacred History," 152; Tricaud, "L'ancien testament," 230–31, 234; Reventlow, *Authority of the Bible*, 216.

41. Hahn and Wiker, *Politicizing the Bible*, 322.

42. Malcolm, "*Leviathan*," 258.

43. Hahn and Wiker, *Politicizing the Bible*, 334–35. In place of allegorical interpretation, like typology, Hobbes preferred the literal sense. Johann Sommerville notes, however, that "where Hobbes parted company with the literal meaning of scripture, it was because the meaning conflicted with what (his own) philosophy had shown to be

it moves from the sign, the external (e.g., flood or Passover), to the deeper, future reality the sign signified (e.g., baptism or Eucharist).[44] Hobbes's exegesis, in contrast, represented a "reversal of typology" or the "inversion of typology," where, rather than the earthly and natural pointing forward to the heavenly and supernatural, he reduced the meaning of supernatural realities to earthly and natural ones in his attempt to discover the original, pure meaning of the texts.

As we have seen, La Peyrère had used non-biblical sources from other nations to supplant the traditional Jewish and Christian notions of human history, especially biblical history. In his exegetical method, Hobbes made a similar move. Hobbes both ridiculed contemporary Catholic practices and attempted to deconstruct earlier biblical ones by linking them genealogically to earlier pagan practices, underscoring foreign corruption (at least in the case of Catholicism). With regard to the NT practice of baptism and its relationship to earlier Jewish rituals, Hobbes mentions that: "This ceremony of the Greeks, in the time that Judaea was under the dominion of Alexander . . . may probably enough have crept into the religion of the Jews."[45] After enumerating numerous such examples, he writes: "If a man would well observe that which is delivered in the histories, concerning the religious rites of the Greeks and Romans, I doubt not but he might find many more of these old empty bottles of gentilism, which the doctors of the Roman Church, either by negligence or ambition, have filled up again with the new wine of Christianity, that will not fail in time to break them."[46]

Scott Hahn and Benjamin Wiker explain how Hobbes's atomistic reductionism appealed to the broader anti-Aristotelian philosophy within the Protestant world of his time. Such anti-Aristotelian, Protestant thought envisioned Aristotelian philosophy as a corrupting force, foreign to

---

true. Hobbes found in history what theory had already proved" (Sommerville, "Hobbes, Selden," 180).

44. Hahn, "Canon, Cult and Covenant," 227–29; Hahn, "Worship in the Word," 132–35; Hahn, *Letter and Spirit*, 19–31; Mazza, *Mystagogy*, 7–13, 16–17, 167–68.

45. *Leviathan* III.41 in Malcolm ed., *Leviathan*, 3:772. Immediately following this sentence, Hobbes carefully includes: "But seeing it is not likely our Savior would countenance a heathen rite, it is most likely it proceeded from the legal ceremony of washing after leprosy." It is not clear which view Hobbes really holds.

46. *Leviathan* IV.45 in Malcolm ed., *Leviathan*, 3:1050. Machiavelli tread this path long before either Hobbes or La Peyrère. See Hahn and Wiker, *Politicizing the Bible*, 137–40.

Christianity and originating in the pagan Greek world; if Athens has nothing to do with Jerusalem, then Catholicism is a corrupt form of Christianity:

> Thus, Hobbes was able to use a common Protestant position as a shield to put forward his materialist philosophy, and in a way that will become an established tenet of modern historical-critical scholarship. Hobbes will argue that all notions of immateriality in the Bible—whether in regard to the human soul or the existence of angels and demons—are the result of the contaminations of Greek philosophy, so that exegesis properly expunges them, leaving only the "original," materialist-friendly substrate. The "critical" aspect of the method is therefore supplied by Hobbes's materialism; the "historical" aspect of the method follows upon the materialist premises, layering the biblical text from early to late in accordance with Hobbes's purposes. Of course, this layering would also appeal to a Protestant assumption that the original and pure church must be recovered from the layers of historical accretions, an assumption that would bring them to embrace the same historical-critical methods (thereby, ironically, serving the cause of Hobbes).[47]

Hobbes was part of the early modern Epicurean revival, so named after the ancient Greek philosopher Epicurus, which entailed the pursuit of beatitude (for Epicurus, a tranquility of an undisturbed mind) here, in this present life, and not after death, in some afterlife.[48] Epicurus reduced reality to physics, to atomic motion. Hobbes, along with Charles Cavendish (William Cavendish's brother), formed part of this informal group of atomists.

---

47. Hahn and Wiker, *Politicizing the Bible*, 300n46. See also Hahn and Wiker, *Politicizing the Bible*, 300, 324, 337, as well as the comments in Levering, *Participatory Biblical Exegesis*, 108–109; Leijenhorst, "Sense and Nonsense," 82–108; Paganini, "Hobbes's Critique," 337–57; Springborg, "Hobbes and Historiography," 68n6; Sorell, "Hobbes's Uses," 88–89, 92. On Hobbes's anti–Aristotelianism (and thus opposition to Catholicism), Tom Sorell explains: "There is more to Hobbes's attack on Aristotle, but the main points are now before us. By locating that attack within a history of mostly heathen schools of philosophy, Hobbes is able from the start to bring Aristotle under discussion as an unbeliever, and therefore as an unlikely source for any true doctrines about salvation. By bringing in the schoolmen and concentrating on the Catholic side of scholasticism, Hobbes is able to tar Aristotle twice over, once by association with heathens, once more by association with the Pope. At the same time, his own materialist doctrine, which would have seemed grotesquely irreligious in another context, is lent credibility, at least for an English Protestant audience, by being presented as anti–Catholic" (Sorell, "Hobbes's Uses," 89).

48. Hahn and Wiker, *Politicizing the Bible*, 293–94, 296–99, 305, 308, 332; Springborg, "Critical Response," 678–79; Springborg, "Hobbes and Epicurean Religion," 161–214; Springborg, "Hobbes's Theory," 61–98; Sorell, "Hobbes's Uses," 87; Pacchi, "Hobbes e l'epicureismo," 54–71.

Through his close friendship with the Epicurean Pierre Gassendi, Hobbes became an important bridge, smuggling Epicurean philosophy into England.[49] Moreover, Hobbes's Epicureanism was linked with his nominalism, all of which supported his political stances.[50]

Hahn and Wiker explain: "Hobbes attempted to reconstitute Christianity itself through an entirely novel exegesis of Scripture that would support the complete subordination of Christianity to the state."[51] His politics may have shifted throughout his career, depending on whom he served, but the fact remains that his philosophy and exegesis served these secular political aims. Patricia Springborg argues that: "Hobbes, a 'pen for hire,' who spent his entire career in the service of the baronial Cavendishes of Derbyshire, was thus occupationally disposed to be as mentally flexible as Laslett's Locke, the Whig pamphleteer who wrote to promote Shaftesbury's causes."[52]

It is not clear precisely whence Hobbes derived his hermeneutic. Was he aware of, for example, La Peyrère's work? This has been an as yet unresolved question. Whereas scholars like Popkin have often assumed that Hobbes probably was aware of La Peyrère's work—and, in fact, likely relied upon it—more recently, scholars like Noel Malcolm have called this into

---

49. Hahn and Wiker, *Politicizing the Bible*, 298–300; Sorell, "Hobbes's Uses," 87.

50. Hahn and Wiker, *Politicizing the Bible*, 303–4; Gillespie, *Theological Origins*, 215, 228, 231–32, 234, 240, 242, 248–50; Callaghan, "Nominalism," 37–55; Springborg, "Hobbes and Historiography," 65, 67. Early on in *Leviathan*, Hobbes writes: "There being nothing in the world universal but names, for the things named, are every one of them individual and singular" (I.4 in *Leviathan*, 2:52).

51. Hahn and Wiker, *Politicizing the Bible*, 286. On the same page, Hahn and Wiker underscore that: "It was through this politicized exegesis that Hobbes became the true father of modern scriptural scholarship. This point must sink in: Hobbes's *secular-political aim defined and determined his exegetical methods,* so that his methods carry forth the secular-political aim whether later exegetes wielding those methods realize it or not." See also Morrow, *Three Skeptics and the Bible*, 85–103, 139–48; Pacchi, "Hobbes e la filologia," 277–92.

52. Springborg, "Critical Response," 369. Writing earlier on the same page, Springborg maintains: "This evidence for Hobbes's reference group corroborates in an indirect way Baumgold's argument in her essay of 2005 that Hobbes and Locke were more political and less metaphysical thinkers than we tend to think, by advancing the argument a further step. There is a simple reason for believing this which is that both were secretaries or courtier's clients engaged by their masters to write position pieces on current policy. Hobbes's Epistles dedicatory are in this respect most revealing, suggesting the political nature of his programme." See also Baumgold, "Hobbes's and Locke's Contract," 289–308, to which article Springborg refers. On Locke's role in the history of modern biblical criticism, see Hahn and Wiker, *Politicizing the Bible*, 425–86; Reventlow, *History of Biblical Interpretation*, 4:51–65.

question.⁵³ Part of the complexity deals with the dating of La Peyrère's arguments concerning Pentateuchal origins in *ST*. Were they sufficiently prior to Hobbes's drafting of the thirty-third chapter of *Leviathan*? Another aspect concerns whether or not Hobbes knew La Peyrère and whether or not their mutual friends (which included François La Mothe le Vayer, Marin Mersenne, Pierre Gassendi, and Samuel Sorbière) discussed La Peyrère's views with Hobbes. Regardless of whether or not Hobbes learned anything from La Peyrère (directly or indirectly), was merely confirmed by La Peyrère's work, or was completely unaware of it, Hobbes, too, like La Peyrère, had a political motivation for his biblical hermeneutic: such a hermeneutic supported his state politics.

The Quest for a Scientific Biblical Hermeneutic: Baruch Spinoza

Baruch Spinoza was born to a Jewish family in Amsterdam in 1632.⁵⁴ After his father's death, Spinoza took control of his father's business, which then went bankrupt. After appealing to the secular authorities in Amsterdam for a legal guardian (still permitted even though Spinoza was 23 years old at the time), the Sephardic Jewish community of Amsterdam excommunicated him. It is unclear from the text of the excommunication what the precise reasons for his expulsion were, but most scholars have assumed theological reasons, likely the seeds which germinated into his mature theological and philosophical thought, as evidenced in his later *Ethica* (*Ethics*) and his *Tractatus Theologico-politicus* (*Theological-Political Treatise*). As with Hobbes's *Leviathan*, Spinoza's *Tractatus Theologico-politicus* is not only a political work, but it also deals in great part with biblical hermeneutics. In it, we find the blueprints of modern biblical criticism.

Spinoza makes clear at the outset of his *Tractatus Theologico-politicus* that the violence he identifies as having religion as the root cause—as in

---

53. Popkin, *History of Scepticism*, 190; Popkin, *Isaac La Peyrère*, 5, 49. For caution here, see Malcolm, *Aspects of Hobbes*, 395–97. See also the discussion in Bernier, *La critique du Pentateuque*, 132–33, 143–44.

54. For biographical information on Spinoza, see Morrow, "Spinoza and the Theo-Political Implications," 374–87; Morrow, *Theology, Politics, and Exegesis*, 16–34; Morrow, *Three Skeptics and the Bible*, 104–38; Hahn and Wiker, *Politicizing the Bible*, 339–93; Reventlow, *History of Biblical Interpretation*, 4:89–110; Nadler, "Bible Hermeneutics," 827–36; Frampton, *Spinoza and the Rise of Historical Criticism*, 121–98; Popkin, *Spinoza*; Nadler, *Spinoza*.

the Thirty Years' War, which ended when he was about 16—is the *raison d'être* of a scientific biblical exegesis like that which he proposes.⁵⁵ Of the trio—La Peyrère, Hobbes, and Spinoza—Spinoza clearly developed the most thorough biblical hermeneutic. Moreover, Spinoza's Hebrew philological abilities far outstripped those of La Peyrère or Hobbes. Richard Simon reported that La Peyrère knew neither Greek nor Hebrew.⁵⁶ Hobbes's Greek was exceptionally good, but the evidence indicates that he knew no Hebrew, at least by the writing of *Leviathan*.⁵⁷ Spinoza knew Greek, and he even wrote a grammar of the Hebrew language.⁵⁸ Nevertheless, it is clear that Spinoza was influenced—or at least encouraged in the same direction—by La Peyrère's work, and may have been influenced by Hobbes, in his biblical criticism, as well.

La Peyrère's book, *Prae-Adamitae* (which was bound together with *Systema Theologicum*), was in Spinoza's library, and it is possible that the two met when La Peyrère visited the Dutch Republic in 1655—the very same year *Prae-Adamitae* was published.⁵⁹ It also seems likely that Spinoza

---

55. See his comments in Spinoza, *Tractatus Theologico-politicus*, preface §4–5, 7. All citations to the Latin text of Spinoza's *Tractatus Theologico-politicus* will be taken from Spinoza, *Œuvres III*. All English translations in this chapter will be taken from Spinoza, *Theological-Political Treatise*.

56. Although it is clear from his private letters that he knew at least some rudimentary Greek, it is possible that he likewise knew some basic fundamental information about Hebrew. See comments in Morrow, *Three Skeptics and the Bible*, 54–84; Nellen, "Growing Tension," 818; Popkin, *Isaac La Peyrère*, 18, 42.

57. This is because of very elementary mistakes he makes, demonstrating that he is not aware of Hebrew. Noel Malcolm indicates that evidence exists that Hobbes probably learned some basic, rudimentary elements of Hebrew after *Leviathan* was published, since he shows knowledge of basic points where before he had made mistakes. See Malcolm, *Aspects of Hobbes*, 413n103.

58. Spinoza, *Compendium Grammatices*. On his Hebrew grammar, see Rodrigues, "Algumas notas," 111–29; Klijnsmit, "Some Seventeenth-Century," 92–96; Klijnsmit, "Amsterdam Sephardim," 144–64; Klijnsmit, "Problem of Normativity," 305–14; Levy, "Problem of Normativity," 351–90; Gruntfest, "Spinoza as a Linguist," 103–28.

59. See chapter 4 in this present volume; Morrow, *Three Skeptics and the Bible*, 10–53, 104–38; Hahn and Wiker, *Politicizing the Bible*, 349; Bernier, *La critique du Pentateuque*, 112, 120–21, 138; Jorink, *Reading the Book of Nature*, 105, 409; Jorink, "Horrible and Blasphemous," 431; Malcolm, *Aspects of Hobbes*, 390; Popkin, *Isaac La Peyrère*, 1, 72, 74, 79, 84–88; Popkin, "Spinoza and La Peyrère," 188–91; Freudenthal, *Spinoza*, 159–60. Eric Jorink writes that: "[Joseph] Scaliger—whether intentionally or not—determined the direction of future inquiry: the scrutiny of the biblical text in the light of other written sources. In this respect, we can regard La Peyrère's *Praeadamitae*, published in the Dutch Republic in 1655, as the new paradigm. Although there were hardly any defenders

knew Hobbes's *Leviathan* in Latin (or Dutch?) prior to completing *Tractatus Theologico-politicus* (1669–1670). Spinoza did not know English, but *Leviathan* was published in Dutch in 1667 and appeared in Latin in 1668. We know he read (and owned a copy of) Hobbes's earlier political work, *De Cive*.[60] Spinoza had many other influences on his work, especially Descartes. Jean Bernier remarks, in fact: "The Spinozist approach to the Bible in the *Tractatus* retains as a foundation the radical doubt of Cartesianism."[61] Francis Bacon's work also appears to have been important to Spinoza. Spinoza not only applied a form of Cartesian doubt to the study of Scripture, but also a Baconian natural history, as it were, of the biblical text.[62] As James Samuel Preus explains: "Like Bacon, Spinoza takes a bottoms-up approach that begins with the data—in this case, all relevant factual information needed as a foundation for understanding the Bible."[63]

Following a history which includes La Peyrère and Hobbes, Spinoza also denied the substantial Mosaic authorship of the Pentateuch but with much more sophisticated arguments than what was found in the former authors.[64] The casting of doubt on traditional attributions of the authorship

---

of Preadamitism in the Dutch Republic, the book was to determine the parameters of discussions of the authority of the Bible, the antiquity of the earth and the status of the history of non–Christian nations for decades" (Jorink, *Reading the Book of Nature*, 409).

60. See chapter 4 in this present volume; Morrow, *Three Skeptics and the Bible*, 10–53, 139–48; Hahn and Wiker, *Politicizing the Bible*, 370, 376n182, 381–83, 385, 388–90; Lagrée and Moreau, Introduction, 14; Nadler, *Book Forged in Hell*, 30–31, 34, 92, 94–96, 119, 188, 190, 193; Bernier, *La critique du Pentateuque*, 112, 120–21; Curley, "Spinoza's Exchange," 13n6; Nelson, *Hebrew Republic*, 151n84; Lorberbaum, "Spinoza's Theological-Political," 170, 172–73, 178–79, 183n11, 184n28; Parkin, "Reception of Hobbes's *Leviathan*," 450–51; Malcolm, *Aspects of Hobbes*, 390–92; Preus, *Spinoza and the Irrelevance*, 14, 30, 30n91, 68n3, 110, 157n8; Elazar, "Spinoza and the Bible," 8–9; Pacchi, "*Leviathan* and Spinoza's *Tractatus*," 577; Schuhmann, "Methodenfragen," 47–86; Osier, "L'herméneutique," 319–47; Gallicet-Calvetti, "In margine," 52–84, 235–63; Sacksteder, "How Much," 25–39.

61. Bernier, *La critique du Pentateuque*, 34 (my translation). See also the comments in Hahn and Wiker, *Politicizing the Bible*, 259, 281, 342–43, 388, 546; James, *Spinoza*, 9–11, 92, 144–47, 150, 155, 218; Beyssade, "Deux latinistes," 55–68; van Bunge, *From Stevin to Spinoza*, especially 34–121; Yovel, *Spinoza and Other Heretics I*, 206; Curley, *Behind the Geometrical*; Curley, "Spinoza's Geometric Method," 151–69.

62. Manrique Charry, "La herencia de Bacon," 121–30; Preus, *Spinoza and the Irrelevance*, 7n19, 24n73, 26n80, 38, 158n9, 159, 159n12, 161–68, 163n20–21, 181, 195; Gabbey, "Spinoza's Natural," 170–72; Donagan, *Spinoza*, 16–17; Zac, *Spinoza*, 29–32.

63. Preus, *Spinoza*, 164.

64. Bernier, *La critique du Pentateuque*, 146–71, 174–76, 188–92; Gibert, *L'invention critique*, 170–73; Kugel, *How to Read the Bible*, 29–31; Gibert, *L'invention de l'exégèse*

of biblical books and the quest for sources underlying the texts became part and parcel of Spinoza's method. He detailed his method, particularly in the seventh chapter of *Tractatus Theologico-politicus*.[65] In summary form, Spinoza constructs an elaborate biblical hermeneutic including the following goals, hermeneutical principles, and stages: (1) construct a "natural history" of Scripture;[66] (2) utilize Scripture alone;[67] (3) "investigate *all* the possible meanings that *every* single phrase in common usage can admit";[68] (4) "gather together the opinions expressed in each individual book and organize them by subject so that we may have available by this means *all* the statements that are found on each topic";[69] (5) "make note of any that are ambiguous or obscure or seem to contradict others";[70] (6) "explain the circumstance of *all* the books of the prophets";[71] (7) uncover every conceivable facet of "the life . . . of the author of each individual book";[72] (8) discover every aspect of the "character . . . of the author of each individual book";[73] (9) find out all of the "particular interests of the author of each individual book";[74] (10) find out who was each biblical book's author;[75] (11) learn when and why each author wrote their book;[76] (12) investigate who the primary audience was for each book;[77] (13) discover

---

moderne, 27–31.

65. Spinoza, *Tractatus Theologico-politicus*, 7.2–18; Morrow, *Three Skeptics and the Bible*, 104–38; Hahn and Wiker, *Politicizing the Bible*, 375–77; Nadler, *Book Forged in Hell*, 134–42; Barthélemy, *Studies in the Text*, 53–57; Gibert, *L'invention*, 161–65; Sinai, "Spinoza and Beyond," 196–203; Levering, *Participatory Biblical Exegesis*, 115–17; Kugel, *How to Read*, 31–32; Frampton, *Spinoza*, 223–29; Gibert, *L'invention de l'exégèse moderne*, 27–31; Dungan, *History of the Synoptic Problem*, 212–13, 234–38; Walther, "Biblische Hermeneutik," 227–29; Yovel, *Spinoza and Other Heretics II*, 14–19; Moreau, "Le méthode," 109–14; Garrido, "El método," 269–81.

66. Spinoza, *Tractatus Theologico-politicus*, 7.2.
67. Spinoza, *Tractatus Theologico-politicus*, 7.2–5.
68. Spinoza, *Tractatus Theologico-politicus*, 7.5.
69. Spinoza, *Tractatus Theologico-politicus*, 7.5.
70. Spinoza, *Tractatus Theologico-politicus*, 7.5.
71. Spinoza, *Tractatus Theologico-politicus*, 7.5.
72. Spinoza, *Tractatus Theologico-politicus*, 7.5.
73. Spinoza, *Tractatus Theologico-politicus*, 7.5.
74. Spinoza, *Tractatus Theologico-politicus*, 7.5.
75. Spinoza, *Tractatus Theologico-politicus*, 7.5.
76. Spinoza, *Tractatus Theologico-politicus*, 7.5.
77. Spinoza, *Tractatus Theologico-politicus*, 7.5.

in what language the books were originally written;[78] (14) find out who received each book after it was written;[79] (15) investigate all of the variant readings in the manuscript tradition;[80] (16) investigate the decisions which canonized the books;[81] (17) be equipped with "a *perfect* knowledge of the Hebrew language";[82] etc.

These areas for investigation are not problems in and of themselves. In fact, they are worthy historical investigations. His starting points, however—like his version of the Protestant assumption of *sola Scriptura* and his advocacy for a "perfect" knowledge of Hebrew—are untenable. On the other hand, the historical hermeneutic which he proposes is not put forward as a realistic program for investigation but rather a "nominalist barrage" of endless details for an investigation which is actually impossible to achieve complete results; complete results of which Spinoza requires in order to proceed to theology.[83] As David Dungan makes clear: "Spinoza and his followers multiplied questions about the physical history of the text to the point that the traditional theological task could never get off the ground."[84] Spinoza himself hints at this in the various places where he mentions the impossibility of many of the tasks he sets forth therein.[85] It should come as no surprise that, like Hobbes, when Spinoza approaches miracles and the supernatural in Scripture's pages, he naturalizes them, demystifying Scripture.[86]

Implicit in the methods La Peyrère, Hobbes, and Spinoza constructed are the acids of skepticism, of methodic doubt. They were political tools, used for a specific end. Their specific political ends (for La Peyrère, supporting Condé's political machinations; for Hobbes, supporting the status quo in England; and for Spinoza, defanging Calvinist politics and gutting the Jewish community which ostracized him in the Dutch Republic) share a general

---

78. Spinoza, *Tractatus Theologico-politicus*, 7.5.
79. Spinoza, *Tractatus Theologico-politicus*, 7.5.
80. Spinoza, *Tractatus Theologico-politicus*, 7.5.
81. Spinoza, *Tractatus Theologico-politicus*, 7.5.
82. Spinoza, *Tractatus Theologico-politicus*, 7.11.
83. Dungan, *History of the Synoptic Problem*, 172. See also the insightful comments in Dungan, *History of the Synoptic Problem*, 239–40, 246, 259.
84. Dungan, *History of the Synoptic Problem*, 172.
85. Spinoza, *Tractatus Theologico-politicus*, 7.12 and 14.
86. Morrow, *Three Skeptics and the Bible*, 104–38; Hahn and Wiker, *Politicizing the Bible*, 364–68; Hammill, *Mosaic Constitution*, 87; Nadler, *Book Forged in Hell*, 76–103; Rosenthal, "Miracles," 231; Garrido Zaragoza, "La desmitificación," 3–45; Malet, *Le traité*, 118.

theo-political agenda: privatizing the Church and her theological claims, creating a secular space, where God is absent or sequestered to the private recesses of an individual's soul—in short, declawing the Church's authority and tradition. This is even the case regardless of whether or not La Peyrère, Hobbes, or Spinoza, are "believers" in any sense of the word. This is the mistake Michael Gillespie, Eric Nelson, and Travis Frampton make in their accounts of theological origins of modernity (Gillespie), modern politics (Nelson), and Spinoza's biblical criticism (Frampton).[87]

These scholars are to be lauded for recognizing such theological motives, influences, and origins, but they do not adequately recognize that such "Erastian" and similar theological agendas are in fact themselves part of the same secularizing theological trend that moves forward from Nominalism to Protestantism, through the Enlightenment, and into Modernity. Certainly, these trends have medieval and theological roots (even some of the tributaries of late medieval scholasticism), but they share a privatizing and secularizing teleology that splits people neatly into public and private selves, handing the public selves ever more into the domain of increasingly secular states.[88] This is one place where the work of Talal Asad and William Cavanaugh, among others, has been so important a corrective.[89]

To early modern historical criticism, as fashioned and practiced by La Peyrère, Hobbes, and Spinoza, we might affix Albert Schweizter's confession about the root of historical Jesus studies, that such a scholarly endeavor was "an aide in the struggle for deliverance from dogma," rather than a Weberian noble scientific quest for unadulterated truth.[90] In light of this concession, we might be tempted to adopt Dungan's analogy of the Trojan Horse from Homer's *Iliad*:

> Modern historical criticism of the Bible was originally forged as a weapon in the furious battle between the Enlightenment and

---

87. See Gillespie, *Theological Origins*; Nelson, *Hebrew Republic*; Frampton, *Spinoza*.

88. For the medieval scholastic roots of Spinoza's thought, see Jakob Freudenthal's much neglected—but very important—1887 essay, "Spinoza und die Scholastik," 84–138. For the medieval Muslim philosophical influence on Spinoza's work, see Fraenkel, "Reconsidering," 213–36; Fraenkel, "Spinoza on Philosophy," 58–81; Djedi, "Spinoza et l'islam," 275–98; Ramón Guerrero, "Filósofos hispano–musulmanes," 125–32; Arnaldez, "Spinoza," 151–74; Wolfson, *Philosophy of Spinoza*.

89. Cavanaugh, *Myth of Religious Violence*; Asad, *Formations of the Secular*; Cavanaugh, "Fire Strong Enough," 397–420; Asad, *Genealogies of Religion*. For an important and fair critique of Cavanaugh's account, see Shadle, "Cavanaugh," 246–70.

90. Schwetizer, *Vom Reimaruz zu Wrede*, 4 (my translation).

the Christian Thrones and Altars of Europe. . . . The inventors of the new historical method first eviscerated the Bible, then secretly packed it with their own values so that, after the defenders of orthodoxy had dragged this strange Trojan horse inside their city, the hidden soldiers could rule the city under the guise of biblical criticism.[91]

The difficulties with the overall hermeneutic of La Peyrère, Hobbes, and Spinoza, are still with us. The danger lies in part in the (often unrecognized) philosophical underpinnings of modern biblical criticism, as Pope Benedict XVI understood so well, as when he wrote of the dangers inherent in hermeneutics, which are secularized, sharply separating reason from faith.[92] Indeed, this was one of the main points in his earlier Erasmus Lecture on the crisis of modern biblical interpretation, where he called for a "Kritik der Kritik," a criticism of Criticism, a historical study of historical criticism itself, whereby such philosophical underpinnings are exposed.[93] When we properly understand the work of La Peyrère, Hobbes, and Spinoza, as well as their reception in the eighteenth century and beyond, the truth in Jon Levenson's statement becomes quite clear: "Historical criticism is the form of biblical studies that corresponds to the classical liberal political ideal. It is the realization of the Enlightenment project in the realm of biblical scholarship."[94]

In short, their aim was to remove authority and tradition from the Church, and this fact remains—regardless of whether or not La Peyrère, Hobbes, or Spinoza were "believers" in any sense of the word. Further examination of the ways in which Enlightenment exegetes like Johann Salomo Semler and Johann Gottfried Eichhorn built upon the work of exegetes like La Peyrère, Hobbes, and especially Spinoza will help us to better understand the ways in which their biblical hermeneutics bear with them a politics. This politically-shaped exegesis is hence not neutral, to be contrasted with the more traditional theological exegesis; rather, it, too, is partisan to the historic church and state conflicts which remain with us today.

---

91. Dungan, *History of the Synoptic Problem*, 148.
92. Benedict XVI, "Verbum Domini," 713–16.
93. Benedict XVI, *Schriftsauslegung im Widerstreit*, 22.
94. Levenson, *Hebrew Bible*, 118.

3

The Brave New World of Seventeenth-Century Biblical Interpretation

IN THE LAST CHAPTER, we discussed Isaac La Peyrère (1596), Thomas Hobbes (1588), and Baruch Spinoza (1632–1677) at some length, situating them in their immediate historical context, in light of their biographies, so as to understand their place within the history of modern biblical scholarship more clearly. In this chapter, we will better situate Hobbes and Spinoza in light of their broader context, within the history of scholarship, focusing greater attention on the philosophical underpinnings of their output. Here we add other significant but much neglected figures into the mix: René Descartes (1596–1650), Fr. Richard Simon (1638–1712), John Locke (1632–1704), and John Toland (1670–1722).[1] With these figures, we continue the first chapter's account of Scott Hahn and Benjamin Wiker in their massive intellectual history, *Politicizing the Bible*.[2]

Thus, in this chapter we begin by turning to Descartes and expositing his role in effecting a great cosmological shift, wherein nature becomes mathematized and geometry emerges as the primary form of rationality. This sets the stage for a secular cosmos, devoid of God and the supernatural, and thus a fully secular biblical hermeneutic can emerge. We can then revisit Hobbes in light of Descartes's great cosmological shift. In contrast to my focus on Hobbes in the prior chapter (and elsewhere),[3] here, my focus is on how Hobbes's contribution to biblical scholarship matters inasmuch as he provides a secularized exegesis that makes sense for an atomist-mechanist worldview. Hobbes is clearly influenced by Descartes

---

1. This chapter is an expansion of about eight pages in my *Theology, Politics, and Exegesis*, 8–15.
2. Hahn and Wiker, *Politicizing the Bible*.
3. See Morrow, *Three Skeptics and the Bible*, 85–103, 147–51.

and Machiavelli, and, as we have seen, his exegesis supports the kind of state Henry VIII created.

Hobbes's political exegesis helps lead to the next figure—namely, Spinoza. Here, in contrast to focusing on the many influences on Spinoza's thought (including Averroës, Machiavelli, Descartes, and Hobbes),[4] I situate him within his early radical Enlightenment context, showing how his work played a crucial role in the later Enlightenment, something that has also been explored in the important work of Jonathan Israel.[5] As we have already seen, Spinoza tried to construct a scientific biblical exegesis which, like Hobbes's hermeneutic and Descartes's philosophy, was an attempt to bring peace to a Europe torn asunder by violence they all identified as fundamentally religious in motivation.

From Spinoza, I turn to another seventeenth-century critic, one who ostensibly critiqued Spinoza, Fr. Richard Simon. As I showed in my previous book, *Theology, Politics, and Exegesis*,[6] Simon took Spinoza's method as a starting point in order to critique him, challenging Protestant notions of *sola Scriptura* and buttressing Catholic tradition. Ironically, Simon in fact extended Spinoza's hermeneutic and ensured its survival among biblical scholars in the future.

After Simon, I examine the work of Locke, illustrating how he built upon the methods of exegesis of Hobbes, Spinoza, and Simon in order to support the politics in which he very actively played a part. After Locke, I conclude this chapter with a look at the work of Toland and the beginning of English Deist biblical exegesis, showing not only how Toland built upon the work of those that came before him (e.g., Machiavelli, Spinoza, and Simon) but also how his conclusions demonstrate that the most radical effects of historical criticism in the nineteenth century were already in place, intrinsic in the methods themselves, by the end of the seventeenth century.

Cosmopolis and the Twilight of the Scriptural World: Descartes and the Mathematization of Nature

Descartes's revolutionary work, although not usually considered in standard histories of modern biblical criticism, was significant in changing the intellectual landscape in which modern biblical criticism would develop in

---

4. Morrow, *Three Skeptics and the Bible*, 104–38.
5. See Israel, *Enlightenment Contested*; Israel, *Radical Enlightenment*.
6. Morrow, *Theology, Politics, and Exegesis*, 35–51.

the seventeenth century and beyond.[7] For our purposes, Descartes is less important for the way he used the Bible than for his forging a hermeneutic of doubt, which ultimately was applied to the Bible, even though Scripture did not really play much of a role in Descartes's philosophy. What he did, however, was create a method at the core of which was doubt or suspicion; its application to Scripture would have profound consequences for the future of biblical criticism.

Descartes fits firmly within the context of what Hahn and Wiker call the "great cosmological shift that occurs in the seventeenth century."[8] In addition to the "modern cosmological shift," which Descartes helped influence, this "father of *modern* philosophy" is also noteworthy because he was a key figure in the new "focus on method" that would produce what Hahn and Wiker aptly refer to as a "'mania' for *method*."[9] If we consider Descartes in the context of the history we recounted in the first chapter, we might say, as Hahn and Wiker do, that, "the new, secular political focus set forth by Marsilius and Machiavelli in the fourteenth and sixteenth centuries would finally have received a cosmological foundation in the seventeenth century. . . . Their politicizing of Scripture could now receive support from a new science of nature."[10]

One of the most significant factors in his biography is the immediate context of the so-called "wars of religion." The violence which engulfed Europe during the sixteenth and seventeenth centuries provides an important but too often neglected context for understanding the purpose behind Descartes's *Discourse on Method*. Descartes's method was in part an attempt to create a universal epistemological method to bring an end to what he and others identified as religious disputes. The idea was that if everyone understood reality in the same way, by recourse to the same philosophical method, they would no longer be divided as thoroughly, and thus there would no longer be a cause for such religious violence. As I showed in *Three*

---

7. In what follows on Descartes, see Hahn and Wiker, *Politicizing the Bible*, 257–84.
8. Hahn and Wiker, *Politicizing the Bible*, 257.
9. Hahn and Wiker, *Politicizing the Bible*, 258.
10. Hahn and Wiker, *Politicizing the Bible*, 258. Of course, we might place the caveat that Marsilius may not have been bent on a secularizing trend as much as Hahn and Wiker depict him in *Politicizing the Bible*, but he may have fit more within the traditional medieval world in which he wrote. It is not entirely clear which is correct.

Skeptics and the Bible, this was also part of Spinoza's hermeneutical project.[11] Descartes's prior account of nature was "entirely mechanistic."[12]

Hahn and Wiker note that there is no evidence of any sort of direct Averroist or Marsilian influence on Descartes, but they include a very useful discussion of what they term "illuminating similarities" between Descartes and both Averroës and Marsilius.[13] In many ways, Descartes's method played an immense role in helping to construct what we think of as modernity, giving birth to a completely new understanding of the cosmos. This cosmological shift or transformation quickly became the matrix in which seventeenth and eighteenth century modern biblical criticism would function. Descartes's proposed epistemological method was an attempt to place "both philosophy and humanity on a firm foundation," unhampered by strife from religious wars.[14]

Hahn and Wiker identify three key ways in which he effects modernity: "the *mathematization*, the *mechanization*, and the *mastery* of nature."[15] Descartes effects this by creating a completely new approach to understanding the nature of mathematics. As Hahn and Wiker explain in more detail:

> Descartes presents a way to unite algebra and geometry so that . . . geometric shapes and relationships can be translated into algebraic formulae, and then an even larger, more comprehensive class of algebraic formulae can be translated back into a *symbolic geometry* capable of representing all relationships of magnitudes . . . as ratios and proportions of lines, thereby creating a *mathesis universalis*. . . . Descartes's brilliance consists in *imposing the theoretical conception upon nature*. . . . [He] self-consciously fashioned a mathematical ontology, stripping everything from nature but homogenous extension so that there could be a simple identity between his *mathesis universalis* and nature. . . . Descartes's revolution consisted in the substitution of mathematical forms for Aristotelian forms as the universals governing particulars. . . . Forms were not done away with; there was merely a substitution of mathematical forms for common-sense forms.[16]

11. Morrow, *Three Skeptics and the Bible*, 106–10.
12. Hahn and Wiker, *Politicizing the Bible*, 264.
13. Hahn and Wiker, *Politicizing the Bible*, 265–66.
14. Hahn and Wiker, *Politicizing the Bible*, 266–67.
15. Hahn and Wiker, *Politicizing the Bible*, 267.
16. Hahn and Wiker, *Politicizing the Bible*, 267–68. Here, Hahn and Wiker explain how Ockham prepared the way for Descartes: "In championing nominalism, Ockham removed the reality of universals that inhered in similar-looking substances, so that

With Descartes's cosmological shift, there was no longer any room for the miraculous, even if Descartes himself believed in God and the miraculous. Descartes may have remained a faithful Catholic, but his followers who picked up his epistemology and carried it forward, shaping modernity, began to apply his methodic doubt to religious faith, God, Scripture, and the miraculous. Spinoza and others who followed in Descartes's path, even as they disagreed with him in some ways, began to apply his methodic doubt to the very pages of Scripture itself. Descartes made this possible, intentionally or unintentionally, by positioning such doubt as a logical consequence of a rational epistemology like his own. This hides, somewhat, the truth of the matter: it was really his epistemology, coupled with his mathetmatization of reality, that made such doubt appear necessary.

As Hahn and Wiker make clear: "The posture of doubt is inseparable from the method *because* it serves to remove the obstacles to Descartes's unique union of mathematization, mechanization, and mastery."[17] This played out in nefarious ways in modern biblical criticism. Hahn and Wiker bring attention to the regrettable but undeniable fact that "the habitual posture of doubt ingrained by following Descartes's method will become the unquestioned beginning point of many of the most prominent scriptural scholars toward the biblical texts."[18]

Hobbes and *Leviathan*

I covered Hobbes's work in more detail in the previous chapter (as well as in *Three Skeptics and the Bible*),[19] but at this point, it is necessary to return to Hobbes to see how his biblical work functioned within the new philosophical and cosmological world that Descartes was helping create and to which

---

nouns like sheep, cow, dog, pig, and so on do not have real referents in nature. There is no common form or species that all sheep as sheep share. . . . Ockham thereby created an intellectual vacuum, removing species-name universals but not supplying anything in their place" (Hahn and Wiker, *Politicizing the Bible*, 268).

17. Hahn and Wiker, *Politicizing the Bible*, 275.

18. Hahn and Wiker, *Politicizing the Bible*, 275. They immediately add, "But the skeptical stance toward the Bible is one side of a two-sided coin, the other being mathematically defined rationality, a mechanical view of nature, and the new goal of the technical mastery of nature that provides a secular substitute for the kingdom of God" (Hahn and Wiker, *Politicizing the Bible*, 275).

19. Morrow, *Three Skeptics and the Bible*, 85–103.

Hobbes himself contributed substantially.[20] Hobbes represents a synthesis of what we have covered thus far in chapter one and three of the present volume. In the words of Hahn and Wiker:

> [Hobbes] unified the purely secular aim of Marsilian and Machiavellian political thought with a secular cosmology needed to support it, and did so through an explicitly nominalist (mathematical-mechanistic) philosophy that focuses on the complete mastery of nature, especially human nature—all of which he put forth in the context of the particularities of the English political scene.[21]

As with Descartes, the context for Hobbes was one of strife—both that of the Thirty Years' War, the last and bloodiest of the so-called European "wars of religion," and the English Civil Wars—thus, his goal, as with Marsilius and Descartes before him, was terrestrial peace.

Hahn and Wiker argued that Hobbes's thought has an important Epicurean background. This claim is not without controversy, but although this background is often overlooked in the literature, there remains merit to such a suggestion. Hahn and Wiker are not completely alone in their assessment here. Notably, Arrigo Pacchi and Patricia Springborg's work have also underscored what they take to be Hobbes's Epicurean context.[22] Hobbes was an intimate friend of the famous early modern Epicurean Fr. Pierre Gassendi. Hobbes thus became an important player in the revival of the "ancient materialist atomism" of earlier figures like Epicurus and Lucretius, for whom terrestrial existence was our only form of life; there is no afterlife on this assumption.[23]

As we have already seen, Hobbes's most important work for getting at his biblical interpretation is his *Leviathan*. *Leviathan* was structured on a Marsilian pattern, as Marsilius had constructed *Defensor Pacis* for a similar goal—namely, earthly peace via a common means and obedience to the temporal ruler (the universal emperor for Marsilius and the local state sovereign for Hobbes). Earlier, we had mentioned an interpretation of Marsilius's work that allows it to fit within the parameters of medieval

---

20. For what follows on Hobbes, see Morrow, *Three Skeptics and the Bible*; Hahn and Wiker, *Politicizing the Bible*, 285–338; Bernier, *La critique du Pentateuque*, especially 27–32, 46–48, 118–20, 126–33, 144–49.

21. Hahn and Wiker, *Politicizing the Bible*, 285.

22. See Springborg, "Hobbes and Epicurean Religion," 161–214; Springborg, "Hobbes's Theory," 61–98; Pacchi, "Hobbes e l'epicureismo," 54–71.

23. Hahn and Wiker, *Politicizing the Bible*, 297. See also Wiker, *Moral Darwinism*.

Christendom as opposed to seeing it as an early secularizing work, as Hahn and Wiker instead argue. Regardless of how Marsilius's *Defensor Pacis* is to be read, Hobbes's *Leviathan* explicitly subsumes the church to the state in a way not possible for the medieval imagination. Hobbes's *Leviathan* contains something quite new. *Leviathan* is roughly divided into two major parts, the first of which "is devoted to a thoroughgoing reductionist account of political life based upon Hobbes's entirely self-contained mechanistic-materialist physics,"[24] and the second of which is a biblical exegetical project used to bolster the conclusions set forth in the first part.

Hobbes's Epicureanism and nominalism reduced all of reality to atomic motion and left little room, if any, to spirits. Even if there was room left for spirits, said spirits are material. For Hobbes: "True science must be a nominalism modeled on Euclidean geometry."[25] As with Machiavelli before him, however, Hobbes understood the necessity of religion in order to maintain political power. He therefore did not eliminate religion altogether but rather sought to erase the fear of consequences beyond physical life and death (such fear in which religion is rooted for Hobbes), beyond what a state sovereign can grant, thus granting the sovereign full control over religion within the realm.

In the second half of *Leviathan*, we find Hobbes's exegetical project wherein he interprets the Bible to support his politics and philosophy, thus placing all temporal and spiritual power in the hands of the civil sovereign and declawing the church of any real authority apart from the state. One key move Hobbes made was to place all virtual interpretive and exegetical authority explicitly in the hands of the sovereign. Hahn and Wiker rightly emphasize: "Hobbes's real goal was not to undermine the authority of Scripture and traditional authorship completely, but to shift the question of authority from the *text and authorship* to the *authority* of interpretation (and hence to the authority of the interpreter, the political sovereign)."[26]

One key to understanding Hobbes's project, which is not mentioned in the rest of Hobbes scholarship but which Hahn and Wiker have correctly identified, is the way that Hobbes presents "the inversion of typology."[27] Hahn and Wiker explain: "The flow of typology, properly understood, is *forward* in the Divine economy, *toward* the culmination in Christ....

---

24. Hahn and Wiker, *Politicizing the Bible*, 299.
25. Hahn and Wiker, *Politicizing the Bible*, 304.
26. Hahn and Wiker, *Politicizing the Bible*, 322.
27. Hahn and Wiker, *Politicizing the Bible*, 334–35.

Hobbes's typology inverted the order, flowing not toward culmination and spiritual transformation, but backward, toward the reduction to some earthly, original meaning."[28] In this inverted typological exegesis, Hobbes hones Machiavelli's method of selectively using pagan sources to understand Scripture and reduces biblical rituals and traditions to "pagan contamination."[29] His exegetical method would be further honed and built upon by others to come.

Spinoza's Scientific Exegesis

As we saw in the last chapter, Spinoza was the most important biblical exegete to come after Hobbes.[30] Spinoza played an often overlooked but central role in laying out a precise historical and philological biblical method, the outline of which would become foundational to historical criticism. His work, however, cannot really be adequately understood without being situated within its broader intellectual context in the seventeenth-century Dutch Republic. Too many scholars relegate Spinoza to an early inconsequential position within the radical Enlightenment. Jonathan Israel, however, has demonstrated the full importance of Spinoza for the future Enlightenment and modernity.[31]

Aspects of Spinoza's biography remain open matters of debate within Spinoza scholarship. The most significant of these surrounds the reasons for Spinoza's excommunication. Richard Popkin's 2004 comments on this matter are still appropriate: "To this day, we are not sure why he was excommunicated and what this actually entailed at the time."[32] Odette Vlessing's work has made a very strong case that Spinoza's excommunication could be explained quite apart from philosophical or theological positions.[33]

28. Hahn and Wiker, *Politicizing the Bible*, 334.
29. Hahn and Wiker, *Politicizing the Bible*, 335.
30. For what follows on Spinoza, see Morrow, *Theology, Politics, and Exegesis*, 16–34; Morrow, *Three Skeptics and the Bible*, 104–38; Hahn and Wiker, *Politicizing the Bible*, 339–93.
31. Israel, *Enlightenment Contested*; Israel, *Radical Enlightenment*.
32. Popkin, *Spinoza*, 27. Popkin's chapter devoted to Spinoza's excommunication is very good for getting a handle on the various scholarly positions (see Popkin, *Spinoza*, 27–38).
33. See Vlessing, "Excommunication," 15–47; Vlessing, "Jewish Community," 195–211; Vlessing, "New Light," 43–75. See also the comments in Kaplan, "Social Functions," 111–55. This is the position I take in Morrow, *Three Skeptics and the Bible*, 110–14, and

Spinoza had very many influences on his work.[34] Such influences certainly include but are not limited to: Descartes, Machiavelli, Maimonides, Averroës, and other Arabic authors.[35] Spinoza's Latin teacher, Franciscus van den Enden, may have been the figure who introduced the works of both Descartes and Machiavelli to Spinoza, although Spinoza may have encountered Descartes even earlier. The first book Spinoza published was on Descartes's philosophy. Three other radical thinkers who were among Spinoza's contemporaries may have also influenced him: Uriel da Costa, Juan de Prado, and Isaac La Peyrère.[36]

Da Costa was in the same Jewish community as Spinoza in Amsterdam. After da Costa's very public humiliation, he committed suicide. In addition to having been a member of Spinoza's community, da Costa was also one of Spinoza's acquaintances, and he was investigated by the leaders of that community the very same year that Spinoza was excommunicated (although de Prado repented within a matter of days, shortly after Spinoza's excommunication). La Peyrère was probably a more crucial influence on Spinoza than da Costa or de Prado, even though he was from France. Spinoza owned La Peyrère's infamous *Prae-Adamitae*, wherein La Peyrère put forward several exegetical and hermeneutical arguments (including the denial of the Mosaic authorship of the Pentateuch) that would sound very much like what Spinoza attempted in his *Tractatus Theologico-politicus*. Moreover, it is possible, as Popkin argued, that Spinoza and La Peyrère were actually together in Amsterdam.[37]

Spinoza was also the intellectual ringleader of sorts for a circle of Dutch Collegiant radicals. In this context, Spinoza's friendships with Adriaan Koerbagh and Lodewijk Meyer become significant, since both of these intellectuals were involved in questions of proper biblical interpretation. All of this is beneficial for understanding how Spinoza's work belongs to

---

it is also the position of Travis Frampton (who follows Vlessing) in his *Spinoza and the Rise of Historical Criticism*.

34. See my more thorough treatment of this in Morrow, *Three Skeptics and the Bible*, 115–20.

35. Much more work still needs to be done on the Arabic (and particularly Muslim) philosophical influences on Spinoza. For now, see Fraenkel, "Reconsidering," 213–36; Fraenkel, "Spinoza on Philosophy," 58–81; Djedi, "Spinoza et l'islam," 275–98; Ramón Guerrero, "Filósofos hispano–musulmanes," 125–32.

36. On La Peyrère's contribution to modern historical criticism, see also Morrow, *Three Skeptics and the Bible*, 54–84; Pietsch, *Isaac La Peyrère*.

37. See Popkin, "Spinoza and La Peyrère," 188–91.

a much broader intellectual current within the Dutch republic, inspired in part by Cartesian philosophy. Regarding Spinoza's friend Lodewijk Meyer's work in relation to Spinoza's, Hahn and Wiker observe: "Meyer's *Philosophia* [*S. Scripturae Interpres*] and Spinoza's *Tractatus* often traveled together in one book, a marriage that made perfect sense. Meyer provided the framework as a prolegomenon, and Spinoza . . . spelled out the full consequences, consequences all the more radical precisely because of Spinoza's radicalizing of Descartes."[38]

Despite Spinoza's reliance upon Meyer, it is necessary to take into account the ways in which Spinoza disagreed with Meyer's work. James Samuel Preus has made a strong case that Meyer is one of the intended targets of Spinoza's *Tractatus*, particularly where Spinoza opposes the exegesis of the medieval Jewish sage, Maimonides.[39] Although Spinoza certainly applies his own radicalized brand of Cartesian skepticism to Scripture, the primary corrosive acid Spinoza employs, in sharp contrast to Meyer, is history. For this, Spinoza is more directly indebted to Francis Bacon than to Descartes. Unfortunately, there is very little treatment in the scholarly literature of Bacon's role in Spinoza's method, despite the fact that Spinoza read Bacon and included a historical method that clearly attempted (even to the point of linguistic parallels to Bacon's work) to bring Bacon's history of nature to bear on a history of Scripture. Much more scholarship needs to be devoted to this neglected influence.[40]

Spinoza's pantheism, his collapsing of God with nature, should be situated within the context of his philosophy, grounded in Euclidean geometry. Moreover, as with Averroës, Spinoza maintained a hierarchy of knowers and of knowledge. He divided knowledge into three types or levels. First, there was experiential knowledge, which he labeled "opinion" or "imagination." The second level of knowledge is "reason," which is mathematical, patterned on geometry. Finally, Spinoza labeled the third type of knowledge "intuition," which is the highest form of knowledge. Much like Averroës, Spinoza thought that most people were only able to attain the first

---

38. Hahn and Wiker, *Politicizing the Bible*, 355.

39. See Preus, *Spinoza and the Irrelevance*, 34-202; Preus, "Hidden Opponent," 361-88.

40. For the role of Bacon on Spinoza, see Morrow, *Three Skeptics and the Bible*, 118-19; Manrique Charry, "La herencia de Bacon," 121-30; Preus, *Spinoza and the Irrelevance*, 7n19, 24n73, 26n80, 38, 158n9, 159, 159n12, 161-68, 163n20-21, 181, 195; Gabbey, "Spinoza's Natural," 170-72; Curley, "Kissinger," 341n35; Donagan, "Spinoza's Theology," 343; Donagan, *Spinoza*, 16-17; Zac, *Spinoza*, 29-37.

level of knowledge—"opinion" or "imagination." This is important to keep in mind when we turn to Spinoza's biblical hermeneutic in his *Tractatus*, for, as Hahn and Wiker explain:

> By identifying God with nature and assuming that the order of nature was identical to the clearest, most certain science of mathematics, Spinoza completely and purposely eliminated supernatural revelation as a possibility. God's essence is *entirely* revealed in nature. He *is* nature; therefore, the highest science, the one that truly grasps God's essence, is mathematical-mechanical natural science.[41]

As with Hobbes and Descartes before him (and, we might add, for Meyer too), the "wars of religion"—particularly the Thirty Years' War—provide the main backdrop for his work. Spinoza desired to create a scientific biblical hermeneutic in his *Tractatus* that would serve the earthly political goal of securing peace between warring religious-political factions. As Hahn and Wiker spell out: "The historical-critical method as originally designed by Spinoza is neither neutral nor scientific, but is rather the form of biblical studies that purposely transforms the Bible to act as a political support to keep order in a secular state."[42]

When we turn to Spinoza's *Tractatus*, we find an important hermeneutical key for correctly reading Spinoza, a key which is so often overlooked by Spinoza scholars. That key is Spinoza's *Ethics*, which he began writing prior to his *Tractatus*.[43] In fact, Spinoza interrupted working on his *Ethics*, which was never published within his lifetime but only posthumously, in order to pen his infamous *Tractatus*, which, as the provocative title of Steven Nadler's recent study indicates, Spinoza's contemporaries considered to be "a book forged in hell."[44] Spinoza's philosophy, as expressed in his then unpublished *Ethics*, makes explicit that which was only implied and ambiguous in his *Tractatus*. In the *Ethics*, Spinoza identifies God with nature; because God *is* nature, miracles are not a possibility.[45] For Spinoza,

---

41. Hahn and Wiker, *Politicizing the Bible*, 362.

42. Hahn and Wiker, *Politicizing the Bible*, 364.

43. No one has made this case as clearly and compellingly as Hahn and Wiker, *Politicizing the Bible*, 362–88.

44. See Nadler, *Book Forged in Hell*.

45. Hahn and Wiker point out: "To those who have not read Spinoza's *Ethics* (the very situation of the first readers of the *Tractatus*), the actual and only possible foundation of the assertion that miracles are impossible—that God *is* nature—was obviously not apparent" (Hahn and Wiker, *Politicizing the Bible*, 365).

"*since* miracles are impossible, *therefore* the scientific exegete must look for another explanation of their common occurrence in Scripture."[46] This is precisely what Machiavelli did before Spinoza and, as Graham Hammill notes, Spinoza was "one of Machiavelli's most perceptive readers."[47]

Spinoza constructs his method in order to make "the highest revelation of Scripture moral," then defines "morality in purely secular terms," thus rendering "revelation superfluous, at least for the 'enlightened.'"[48] Within this overall project, one of the key shifts Spinoza effected, which would continue in the later historical-critical exegesis that followed in his trail, was to move from any notion of "truth" within the text, to a focus on "meaning."[49] Spinoza then brought up "a seemingly endless list of historical questions that must be answered before the exegete can discover the meaning of the text."[50] He thus hoped to stop theology from entering into the political realm by rendering such theology virtually impossible or, at most, private. Hahn and Wiker summarize the import of Spinoza's project:

> Democracy eliminates persecution by eliminating the distinction between orthodoxy and heterodoxy, wisdom and foolishness. Those who are highest on the Averroistic hierarchy, the philosophers, are protected from those who are lowest, the vulgar, by the public pretense that both philosophy and theology have been democratized. Yet, ironically, Spinoza takes away with one hand what he offers with the other, by making the analysis of Scripture possible only to the highly educated, the elite exegetes who are well versed in the original languages, history, literary forms, etc. To keep the elite from turning against the philosophers, Spinoza fashions an exegetical method that produces the conclusions that reduce Scripture to a merely moral prop for civil order, one that allows the greatest freedom for philosophy. In fact, since Spinoza's philosophy ultimately defines the method, then the applied method serves to reaffirm Spinoza's philosophy even without the exegete's own knowledge or consent.[51]

---

46. Hahn and Wiker, *Politicizing the Bible*, 365.
47. Hammill, *Mosaic Constitution*, 22.
48. Hahn and Wiker, *Politicizing the Bible*, 369.
49. Hahn and Wiker, *Politicizing the Bible*, 373–75.
50. Hahn and Wiker, *Politicizing the Bible*, 375.
51. Hahn and Wiker, *Politicizing the Bible*, 387–88.

SEVENTEENTH-CENTURY BIBLICAL INTERPRETATION

Richard Simon's Critical History

Richard Simon's scholarship built on what came before, even as he attempted to mount a response to it, and yet his scholarship and motives appear somewhat ambiguous.[52] Hahn and Wiker even entitle their chapter devoted to Simon's contribution to modern biblical criticism, "The Ambiguous Richard Simon." This ambiguity arises both from Simon's ostensible purpose for writing coupled with the content of what he wrote. Simon's work was explicitly an attempt at defending the Catholic tradition from contemporary challenges, e.g., Spinoza. It does not take long reading his work, however, to recognize its kinship with Spinoza's project and the many ways in which he built upon and took Spinoza's own method forward.[53]

Simon appeared to be defending the Catholic tradition against those who were criticizing it, like Calvinists. Simon used the very same sorts of arguments Spinoza had used prior to make the Protestant principle of *sola Scriptura* untenable. In doing this, however, Simon not only left the textual problems Spinoza identified alone, but rather expanded their scope, adding to them significantly. Simon likewise followed his fellow Oratorian La Peyrère, who had been his friend. La Peyrère was a lay Oratorian after his conversion to Catholicism, and Simon was an Oratorian priest prior to being expelled from the Oratory. Hahn and Wiker emphasize the novelty (within the Catholic tradition) of Simon's approach:

> As it developed, the Catholic position in regard to Scripture's seeming imperfections was that what seemed disunited and imperfect, proved upon humble, faithful, and prayerful reading—guided by the Holy Spirit and Tradition—to be whole and harmonious, containing hidden perfections under seeming imperfections. Various ways arose to explain apparent imperfections: exegetes had recourse to a complex account of divine accommodations, to literal and spiritual senses, and even to the notion of purposely-placed divine stumbling blocks in the text to trip up the prideful and draw the humble to closer examination. Against this, Simon accepted

---

52. For what follows on Simon, see Morrow, *Theology, Politics, and Exegesis*, 35–51; Hahn and Wiker, *Politicizing the Bible*, 395–423; Barthélemy, *Studies in the Text*, especially 58–81; Bernier, *La critique du Pentateuque*, especially 33–41, 44–47, 49–69, 71–114, 117–26, 162–67, 186–208, 210–12, 214–16, 222–24, 277–79, 281–84; Müller, *Richard Simon*; Müller, *Kritik und Theologie*; Stroumsa, "Richard Simon," 89–107; McKane, *Selected Christian Hebraists*, 111–50; Hazard, *La crise*, 125–36.

53. See also the comments in Barthélemy, *Studies in the Text*, 60–62; Mirri, *Richard Simon*, 29–84; Auvray, "Richard Simon," 201–14.

the surface incongruities at face value—even rejoiced in them—so that the need for *traditio* became absolute.⁵⁴

One problem is that Simon's use of tradition appeared arbitrary.

In his *Histoire critique du Vieux Testament* as well as in his *Histoire critique du text du Nouveau Testament*, Simon, very much in line with Spinoza, "shifted the focus of biblical studies from the substance of the text to the history of the text."⁵⁵ One significant move Simon makes, which would develop more completely in the later history of historical-criticism (and particularly form criticism), is to posit "a layered editorial history" for Scripture.⁵⁶ Thus emerged one necessity of a skilled scholarly exegete in order to make sense of the tattered threads of Scripture. Indeed, Simon seems to imply that "only a scholar could plumb the depths of the text."⁵⁷

John Locke and the Politicization of the Bible

John Locke is summarily ignored in works on the history of biblical interpretation, and yet, his work is significant, as Hahn and Wiker's volume demonstrates.⁵⁸ The English Civil Wars provided one of the most important contexts for Locke's life, political intrigues, political philosophy, and work in biblical interpretation. Parliament's rebellion against the king "was neither simply an economic rebellion, nor a political rebellion, nor a religious rebellion, for all three were inextricably bound together, as inseparable in the minds and hearts of all parties as it was in their lives."⁵⁹ Locke came from a family representing "the new propertied class," which sided with English Parliament.⁶⁰ The first of England's Civil Wars began when Locke was a mere ten years old, or thereabouts. When he was a teenager at Westminster, the Second English Civil war began. After the Third English Civil War, an incredibly chaotic time, Locke was a student at the University of Oxford. He lived during very tumultuous times in the history of England.

---

54. Hahn and Wiker, *Politicizing the Bible*, 398.
55. Hahn and Wiker, *Politicizing the Bible*, 404.
56. Hahn and Wiker, *Politicizing the Bible*, 405–6.
57. Hahn and Wiker, *Politicizing the Bible*, 413.
58. For what follows on Locke, see Hahn and Wiker, *Politicizing the Bible*, 425–86.
59. Hahn and Wiker, *Politicizing the Bible*, 427.
60. Hahn and Wiker, *Politicizing the Bible*, 426–27.

Locke was indelibly marked by the violence he witnessed during this time and the political tumult that ripped across England. Moreover, he devoured Hobbes's famous political work *Leviathan*, which had a profound impact on his thought. Robert Boyle of the Royal Society, an English Epicurean, also seems to have influenced Locke. Like Hobbes before him, Locke found himself in exile for fear of his life. Locke was followed by spies throughout his exile, but he also served as a spy of sorts, which was a normal role for diplomatic secretaries, his position for the Elector of Brandenburg. Locke apparently was even involved in the Rye House Plot, an attempt to assassinate King Charles II.[61]

Locke befriended the radical Jean Le Clerc and moved in a circle of radical intellectuals while he resided in the Dutch Republic during his exile, only a few years after Spinoza died. There he read Spinoza and Richard Simon, absorbing their works. He even owned two copies of Simon's critical history on the Old Testament. Locke not only travelled freely among such radical intellectuals but also initiated a regular small gathering of these free thinkers, which "was even more . . . [radical] than the circle that had gathered around Spinoza."[62]

Locke's works must be situated in this radical intellectual context in order to understand his biblical hermeneutic, e.g.: *Epistola de Tolerantia*; *An Essay Concerning Human Understanding*; *First Treatise of Government*; *Second Treatise of Government*; *The Reasonableness of Christianity*; and *A Paraphrase and Notes on the Epistles of St. Paul*.[63] Hahn and Wiker point out that the first of these documents, the *Epistola*, is "not an abstract treatise, but a plea for toleration to an as yet unstable government in England."[64] As did Spinoza, Locke asserted that the Bible at heart can be boiled down to a moral code. As Hahn and Wiker explain, for Locke: "Rather than Scripture taking believers into the heart of profound mystery, where the actual *events* of sacred history reveal, as types, eternal and supernatural truths, the Bible became a kind of morality manual that, at its best, illustrated merely rational moral truths."[65] Locke maintained that religious toleration dictates a non-religious (secular) power (government), with

---

61. Ashcraft, *Revolutionary Politics*.
62. Hahn and Wiker, *Politicizing the Bible*, 444.
63. Locke's *Paraphrase* covers Gal, 1–2 Cor, Rom, and Eph.
64. Hahn and Wiker, *Politicizing the Bible*, 445.
65. Hahn and Wiker, *Politicizing the Bible*, 447.

the authority to rule the people, thus privatizing religion, relegating it completely to a private sphere.

Locke's *Essay Concerning Human Understanding*, fits completely within his overarching political plan, as Hahn and Wiker note: "The *Epistola*, the *Essay*, and the *Two Treatises* as well, are all part of Locke's unified project. The goal of the *Essay* . . . was (at least in significant part) to maximize the realm of reason and minimize the realm of faith."[66] In *An Essay Concerning Human Understanding*, Locke privatizes religious faith, utilizing a form of Cartesianism. In Hahn and Wiker's words: "Locke tried to effect a union of the rationalism of Descartes and the empiricism of Boyle, based on the atomist materialism of both (as shared by Galileo, Hobbes, and Newton as well."[67]

As one might expect in such a work, Locke examined the essence of human reason. His work placed severe limits on reason, but then, under this new mathematical rationality, Locke claimed reason, newly redefined, had a further reach than before. Reason, in this understanding, pertained to notions which were both clear and distinct. On account of such precision, newly mathematized reason was the arbiter of divine revelation. When reason encounters any notion that is unable to be detected with the senses, then it is not within the realm of reason, it is irrational. Hahn and Wiker claim that, with Locke: "The principle of *sola scriptura* was therefore transformed into the principle *sola ratio*."[68] Writing further, Hahn and Wiker point out "a direct connection between Locke's epistemology and his Averroistic plan for political tolerance"[69]:

> Reducing the status of revelation to the lowest kind of probability could become a scholarly project (muck akin to Spinoza's strategy of placing endless obstacles before the exegete), one that used the scholarship of those like Richard Simon to undermine the credibility of the text, thereby affirming the need for political tolerance. Yet, at the same time, these exegetical endeavors could provide at least a thin theism, largely constrained to affirming morality, so as not to remove the necessary help that religion gave to maintaining order in society.[70]

---

66. Hahn and Wiker, *Politicizing the Bible*, 450. On the same page, they clarify: "Not undermine [faith], but minimize, since as Locke has already made clear, political order demands religious beliefs, albeit tamed and firmly circumscribed."

67. Hahn and Wiker, *Politicizing the Bible*, 450.

68. Hahn and Wiker, *Politicizing the Bible*, 452.

69. Hahn and Wiker, *Politicizing the Bible*, 455.

70. Hahn and Wiker, *Politicizing the Bible*, 455.

In his *First Treatise of Government*, Locke presented a vision of the individual that was quite at odds with notions of the family up to that time and which would prove highly influential in the West. Here, the rights—and thus the authority—of the individual fundamentally usurped those previously held within family structures. Hahn and Wiker underscore how:

> This displacement signaled the historical shift that Locke himself was trying to effect, from political rule by family (monarch, nobility, father), to political rule by property; more particularly, from the kind of rule that defined pre-Civil War England, to the rule by the propertied class in Parliament that came (after a significant struggle) to define post-Civil War England.[71]

In his *Second Treatise of Government*, Locke completed his project begun in his *First Treatise*—namely, the grounding of rights in the right to property, which became for Locke the most basic right. Hahn and Wiker suggest that Locke's argument might be viewed "justly" as "a concise scriptural vindication of Bacon's project to conquer nature for the sake of this-worldly comfort, and a crib of Boyle's aims for the Royal Society."[72]

Locke's role in the so-called Glorious Revolution is not insignificant in this context. After the Rye House Plot failed, the English crown, on many occasions, attempted to capture Locke and bring him back to England for trial and punishment. Meanwhile, Locke was busy plotting a coup which would bring down King James II and place William of Orange in his stead. After the success of the Glorious Revolution, Locke was able to return to England a hero.

In addition to his more clearly political works, Locke also wrote more directly on the Bible. His works in this domain attempted to support his political agenda by further privatizing religious faith, much in the way Spinoza had before him. Locke's *The Reasonableness of Christianity* was a defense of his claim that the only faith requirement the Bible puts forward is in Jesus's messianic claim. Such an argument, like Spinoza's biblical hermeneutic and Descartes's epistemology, would remove any cause for religious violence. Such public ethics or civil morality would be the central point for Locke as prior with Spinoza. Hahn and Wiker sum up Locke's entire interpretive goal: "Jesus was reduced to being the Messiah so He could be a lawmaker-king, a miracle worker who confirmed the authority of morality for those

---

71. Hahn and Wiker, *Politicizing the Bible*, 460.
72. Hahn and Wiker, *Politicizing the Bible*, 463.

incapable of philosophical demonstration.... [Locke's] main interest seems to be the utility of the Bible for keeping political order."[73]

When we turn to Locke's work on the Pauline epistles, we see how Locke argued for a de facto *sola Scriptura* position. He exhorted would-be Pauline interpreters to eschew any recourse to read biblical commentaries on Paul and instead only read Paul's letters apart from any interpretive traditions. In addition, in regard to his overarching biblical hermeneutic, he warned of reading Scripture as a canonical whole. For Locke, individual books of the Bible must be read on their own and not in light of the other books of Scripture. One glaring irony of this entire line of reasoning, especially his caution against using commentaries, is that such admonitions are found in Locke's very own *commentary*! His arguments proved influential and prepared "the way for the later exegetical emphasis ... on understanding the New Testament primarily as a witness to an early split between Judaizing and non-Judaizing factions."[74]

John Toland's Critique of Priestcraft

John Toland's work built on the history covered thus far and took it into the eighteenth century, in the world of English Deism.[75] Toland's exegesis demonstrates that some of what would flourish as historical criticism in the nineteenth century was already expressed more than a century earlier. Moreover, as Hahn and Wiker maintain: "The radical conclusions of the historical-critical method were built into the method itself."[76] A number of Toland's works make this clear, e.g., *Letters to Serena*; *Pantheisticon*; *Clidophorus, or Of the Exoteric and Esoteric Philosophy*; *The Life of John Milton*; *Christianity not Mysterious*; and *Nazarenus*.

Toland's *Letters to Serena* (1704) articulates a position very much like that bequeathed by the Latin Averroist tradition and Machiavelli, wherein, for Toland, the more enlightened—like philosophers—have a greater facility for certain truths but should use the lower level "truths," like those of religion, to exert proper control over the majority of people. This same line of thought comes through in Toland's later *Pantheisticon* (1720). Again, the point of such religious dissembling on the part of the philosophers was to

73. Hahn and Wiker, *Politicizing the Bible*, 472.
74. Hahn and Wiker, *Politicizing the Bible*, 480.
75. For what follows on Toland, see Hahn and Wiker, *Politicizing the Bible*, 487–541.
76. Hahn and Wiker, *Politicizing the Bible*, 487.

help protect themselves and create a safe society among the less enlightened people, who formed the majority of society.

Toland's *Clidophorus* (1720) furthered this discussion, begun sixteen years earlier in *Letters to Serena* and earlier that same year in *Pantheisticon*, with a sort of Averroist double truth. In *Clidophorus* his concerns were much more over self-preservation. Like Spinoza, Toland assiduously read Machiavelli's works, but unlike Machiavelli, who lauded clerical hypocrisy in *The Prince*, Toland criticized it unabashedly. From Toland's perspective: "Priests prey upon the ignorance of the vulgar, spinning the people's superstition into gold to put in their own pockets, and concealing their ruses by declaring them 'Mysteries.'"[77] Toland wished to create a more public theology that would be grounded in rewritten mythology, where everything was reduced to the natural; the concept of supernatural would no longer be necessary and could thus be dispensed with.

As with Locke, Toland lived in the Dutch Republic and fraternized with "the most radical of intellectual circles."[78] Moreover, just as Locke was no mere theoretician but also actively engaged in the politics of his day, so too was Toland. Toland was a significant defender of the Hanoverian succession. As Hahn and Wiker highlight, Toland "desired to affect the political order" and, at the same time, had become financially desperate.[79] Toland "took it upon himself personally to educate the House of Hanover in his most radical ideas, as a kind of Platonic philosopher, educating a future king or queen in the new civil theology," and he "began his intimate (if short-lived) relationship with Sophia [of Hanover] and her daughter, Sophie, the queen of Prussia."[80] Despite the fact that he was ultimately unsuccessful here, Toland had "conceived the Hanoverian succession as the political means by which a new civic religion could be instantiated in England, one rerooted in pantheism but wearing the public face of a radically reformed Christianity."[81]

At the time of Toland's stay in the Dutch Republic, there was a massive distribution of clandestine skeptical literature circulating in the Dutch Republic, specifically in the sorts of radical intellectual circles in which Toland and Locke frequented. Toland was intimately involved in

77. Hahn and Wiker, *Politicizing the Bible*, 493.
78. Hahn and Wiker, *Politicizing the Bible*, 498.
79. Hahn and Wiker, *Politicizing the Bible*, 504.
80. Hahn and Wiker, *Politicizing the Bible*, 504.
81. Hahn and Wiker, *Politicizing the Bible*, 522.

such trafficking as an important carrier of such clandestine literature. He mastered the art of "reconstructing an existing text to make it a bearer of revolutionary ideas."[82] This included an English translation of Giordano Bruno's pantheistic *Spaccio de la bestia trionfante*. Bruno's text "condemns all revealed religions in the name of reason, but does so under the guise of condemning pagan religion."[83]

Toland followed in the footsteps of earlier figures we covered, like Machiavelli and Spinoza, replacing the supernatural in the Bible with the merely natural. Thus there were no real miracles, according to Toland; such mysteries were political subterfuge, examples of priestcraft. The Bible, he believed, should be read as any other ancient text. Moreover, as with Spinoza's friend Meyer, Toland understood reason as sufficient for biblical interpretation. Furthermore, Toland asserted that priests were unnecessary in true religion since there was nothing beyond the natural for them to mediate.

Much of what Toland argued would profoundly shape the later development of modern historical biblical criticism in the eighteenth and nineteenth centuries, as it moved from England to Germany. Toland would "reformulate history in terms of degeneration from rational religion to priestly superstition."[84] Elaborating, Hahn and Wiker explain: "Toland was himself not merely another moderate English divine continually blurring Christianity's sharp doctrinal edges with Latitudinarianism until it shaded into the gentleman's religion of deism—but rather part of a larger, radical international intellectual movement that had rejected Christianity."[85]

The ways in which succeeding generations of scholars and intellectuals built upon the prior work of those that came before is pronounced. In the past few chapters, we have looked at some of this history in light of the philosophies and politics of the times in which each figure lived and how they gave shape to their biblical interpretation. In the next chapter, we will take a bird's eye view of the history of biblical interpretation, looking at how biblical interpretation developed in light of changing notions of biblical inspiration, from the earliest centuries to the modernist controversy of Roman Catholicism at the dawn of the twentieth century.

---

82. Hahn and Wiker, *Politicizing the Bible*, 508.
83. Hahn and Wiker, *Politicizing the Bible*, 515.
84. Hahn and Wiker, *Politicizing the Bible*, 533.
85. Hahn and Wiker, *Politicizing the Bible*, 505.

4

A Genealogy of Catholic Notions of Inspiration

ON SEPTEMBER 8, 1907, Pope St. Pius X condemned Modernism as the "synthesis of all heresies" in *Pascendi Dominici Gregis*, his papal encyclical on the doctrines of the Modernists.[1] Scholars sometimes date the Modernist crisis to St. Pius X's promulgation of this encyclical. The crisis identified in *Pascendi*, however, reaches back into the nineteenth century and even earlier. Scholars of the controversy over Modernism typically emphasize several general trends within nineteenth and twentieth-century Catholic theology as the root issues involved in the debate: the focus on subjectivity in theological experience and especially the turn to the history of doctrinal development as opposed to engaging in theology as if doctrine was merely propositional. I argue, however, that at the root of the Modernist crisis lies the biblical question. The full-flowering of the biblical question within Catholicism—that is, the issue of modern biblical criticism and its relationship to Catholic theology—arose with Modernism. At heart, Modernism was about the full-scale appropriation of the modern historical critical method into Catholic biblical interpretation, but it was also much more than this. Modernism gave birth to the biblical question in the Catholic world.

This question over the role of modern biblical criticism, which has by and large come to be identified with the historical critical method, is of fundamental importance for contemporary Catholic theology and exegesis. The near hegemonic status of historical criticism in the academy, with its attendant atrophy of theological exegesis, has occasioned a crisis in Catholic biblical scholarship. This crisis involves the near absolute separation of Catholic biblical scholarship from Catholic systematic theology,

---

1. Pius X, *Papal Encyclicals*, 89.

wherein both ignore the other as though they were unrelated. At most, Catholic systematic theologians will occasionally rely on a truncated appropriation of the "assured" conclusions of historical criticism. Meanwhile, Bible scholars, in their pretentious claims of objectivity and neutrality, often remain blind to the particular philosophical, theological, and political commitments to which their methods remain wedded, thus prompting Joseph Cardinal Ratzinger to call for a "criticism of criticism"—which is the inspiration for this present book.[2]

It is beyond dispute that Catholic theology demands careful attention to history when it comes to biblical interpretation. Thus, some form of historical criticism is certainly necessary within Catholic biblical exegesis. If we take the Incarnation of Jesus seriously and understand the Catholic doctrine of Scripture's dual authorship, which includes the human authors as very real instrumental authors, we cannot avoid historical interpretation. The problem is when the canons of modern history take precedent in one's biblical hermeneutic. Magisterial teaching, the doctrine of the Church, and faith must always remain primary. Unfortunately, much of contemporary Catholic biblical scholarship makes it difficult for the study of Scripture to be the "soul of theology."[3] A resolution to this problem is what we must seek tirelessly.

This present chapter unfolds in three parts. In the first portion, I explain how the Modernist crisis was the birth of the biblical question in the Catholic world. I then proceed, in the second section, to show how problems with Modernist appropriations of historical criticism continue to plague Catholic biblical studies and theology. Finally, in the remainder of the chapter, I suggest the importance of the Catholic doctrine of biblical inspiration for helping to unite faith and reason, tradition and history, in Catholic biblical interpretation. My overarching argument is that the Catholic doctrine of the dual authorship of Scripture requires a hermeneutic of faith where Catholic faith does not diminish or impair reason but rather empowers it.

---

2. See Ratzinger, "Biblical Interpretation," 91–126.

3. *Dei Verbum* 24 in Tanner, *Decrees*, 980. The Latin texts of all citations from the documents of the Ecumenical Councils are taken from Tanner, *Decrees*.

The Modernist Crisis and the Biblical Question

Concerns over the use of modern biblical criticism in Catholic biblical exegesis predate the Modernist crisis by centuries. Indeed, the roots of historical criticism can be traced back at least as far as medieval Nominalist philosophy, if not earlier, in the polemical works of various Roman philosophers and Gnostic thinkers. But it is only in the nineteenth century that we see historical criticism come of age, and, in the Catholic world, we find its most complete appropriation in the works of Modernists like Alfred Loisy.[4] Hence, it is my contention that the Modernist crisis was fundamentally about the appropriation of modern historical criticism into Catholic biblical scholarship and, moreover, gave birth to the biblical question in the Catholic world. By the very launching of the biblical question, the Modernist crisis and its immediate historical preface initiated Magisterial teaching on biblical inspiration. In order to understand how the Modernist crisis gave birth to the biblical question, we need to take a brief look at the development of the historical critical method that we have already covered in this book, in *Theology, Politics, and Exegesis*, and in *Three Skeptics and the Bible* in light of the changing notions of biblical inspiration and see its entrance into the Catholic world. Thus, we will better be able to understand the politics which gave rise to the historical critical method and the Modernist crisis.[5]

Inspiration, Interpretation, and Theo-Political Polemics

Early Christian and Jewish interpretations, from the beginning, operated within the parameters of certain basic assumptions. James Kugel identified four of these fundamental assumptions, which I quoted at length in *Three Skeptics and the Bible*.[6] First, virtually all Christian and Jewish biblical interpreters understood Scripture to be mysterious. That is, it was not often immediately clear what the text meant. If the text read one thing, it might actually intend to communicate something else entirely. Secondly, Christian and Jewish interpreters understood Scripture to be something

---

4. See Morrow, *Alfred Loisy*.
5. I have summarized much of this history in Morrow, *Three Skeptics and the Bible*, 10–53.
6. Morrow, *Three Skeptics and the Bible*, 11–12.

relevant for their present moment. That is, they viewed Scripture as intended to teach them points that were applicable to their lives, about how they were to live and act as faithful Christians and Jews. For these ancient interpreters, the point of Scripture was not primarily as a record of history but rather a unified story about God and about how to live. Third, Christian and Jewish interpreters were convinced that Scripture was true, that it was consistent, and that it was free from errors, contradictions, and such when understood properly. Fourth, such Christian and Jewish interpreters understood Scripture ultimately to be from God; God was its author.[7]

Already in antiquity, the above assumptions of Christian and Jewish interpreters received challenges from various intellectuals and groups bent on eroding their faith. The Pentateuch's origins were often of special focus because of its record of God intervening in the history of Israel to give the Ten Commandments and of his election of Israel from among the nations. These date even from before the rise of Christianity, with the pre-Gnostic group known as Nasarenes.[8] In Roman antiquity, Porphyry, a neo-Platonic philosopher, was perhaps the best-known critic of Christianity and Judaism of his age. He challenged a number of traditions regarding the origin of biblical books, from the Book of Daniel to the Pentateuch.[9] Ultimately, most of these critiques were directed against Christian and Jewish claims of the divine origin of their Scriptures.

In the medieval Muslim world, polemicists like Ibn Hazm and philosophers like Ibn Rushd (Averroës) followed suit. Ibn Hazm used his knowledge of language and history to attack Jewish and Christian Scriptures and, in particular, Jewish and Christian notions of divine inspiration. Ibn Hazm wanted to eliminate all forms of spiritual interpretation, and his work spread far and wide.[10] Averroes, strongly influenced by Ibn Hazm, was even more important in the history of modern biblical criticism because he placed philosophy and reason as judge over faith and theology.[11]

Averroism spread throughout the Latin West at a rapid rate and soon was present through significant universities, e.g., the University of Padua.

---

7. Kugel, *How to Read the Bible*, 14–16. See also O'Loughlin, "Controversy over Methuselah's Death," 182–225.

8. Yamauchi, *Gnostic Ethics*, 60.

9. Kofsky, *Eusebius*, 30.

10. Ljamai, *Ibn Hazm et la polémique*, 145–96; Pulcini, *Exegesis as Polemical Discourse*, 57–96; Lazarus-Yafeh, "Some Neglected Aspects," 61–84; Abu Laila, "Ibn Ḥazm's Influence," 103–15.

11. Arnaldez, *Grammaire et théologie*, 319; Asín Palacios, *Abenházam II*, 74, 74n105.

As we have seen, Scott Hahn and Benjamin Wiker argue that this Averroism entered the realm of biblical interpretation with the figure of Marsilius of Padua, who placed the state's authority over the Church. Although it is not clear if Marsilius was an Averroist, he almost certainly would have learned Averroism while studying at the University of Padua. Marsilius's contemporary William of Ockham's exegesis was similar; for both Marsilius and Ockham, there could be no spiritual interpretation. Even if neither were Averroists, the Nominalism inspired by Ockham was disseminated throughout European universities, not merely in Oxford but also Paris, Heidelberg, etc.[12] Much of the biblical work in which Marsilius and Ockham engaged, however, was tied to the politics of Ludwig of Bavaria, under whose protection they lived. Notably, Ludwig was in conflict with Pope John XXII, as we have already seen.[13]

These very early examples of biblical exegetes exemplify polemics that are both theological and political. They are theological because they address biblical interpretation which has long-reaching implications for all aspects of theology. In some instances, matters of theological importance seem to be of primary concern. Political commitments, however, are present at every stage of the journey. The earliest polemics cannot be separated from the politics of the Roman Empire. When we reach the medieval Muslim literature, particularly the figure of Ibn Hazm, we encounter the politics of the Muslim caliphate structure and the concern over non-Muslims within that governmental structure. With Marsilius and Ockham, we see the concern over temporal authority, which they contended resided in state rulers. Ockham's insistence on and articulation of evangelical poverty may have been sincerely theologically motivated, but practically speaking, Ockham's view would attempt to take property and wealth out of the hands of the Church and place them squarely with state rulers who were often in conflict with the pope.

Throne vs. Altar in Biblical Interpretation

The conflict between state rulers and the Church would only increase as the centuries went by. Such a reading might be anachronistic when applied to the medieval world of the twelfth and thirteenth centuries, but by the

---

12. Minnis, "Material Swords," 292–308; Rosenthal, "Heinrich von Oyta," 178–79, 182, 183n5; Troilo, "L'averroismo," 47–77.

13. Miethke, "Der Kampf Ludwigs," 39–74; Nehlsen, "Die Rolle Ludwigs," 285–328.

time of the Renaissance and later Reformation, such a conflict between church and state begins to emerge. In many ways, the Renaissance period saw the development of new scholarly tools in philology and textual criticism that would place the study of Scripture on a firm footing. And yet, it was also during this time period that traditional authority was replaced by the authority of specialists. Renaissance scholarship continued a trend, already present in Ockham, of elevating the scholar over the Magisterium. We see this in the foundational work of Lorenzo Valla and especially Niccolò Machiavelli.[14]

The work of renaissance philologists continued through the Protestant Reformation. The Reformation emphasized the literal sense and attacked Catholic notions of a spiritual sense, thus helping push biblical interpretation into its future critical mode that would eschew recourse to spiritual interpretation. In line with this trajectory—and perhaps most obviously—the Protestant Reformers attempted to dismantle any sense of the Catholic magisterium as an authority in matters of biblical interpretation.[15] And yet, the Reformation itself was enmeshed in the violent transformation of the political realm that was happening at that time. Feudal space throughout Europe was disappearing as centralized states emerged in the seventeenth century, building on trends stretching back centuries. Full-blown church and state conflicts were born in these transformations of the political order.[16] European state rulers attempted to justify their opposition to the papacy. Regions which remained Catholic through the Reformation often had prior concordat agreements, limiting the pope's arm within their realm, whereas the Protestant Reformation was most successful where no such agreements had been secured and where rulers hence needed Protestant theology to justify their politics.[17] The English Reformation proved the paradigm, wherein all opposing forces were put down violently by the state, which, in turn, drove support for reform measures.[18]

The most significant and radical changes within the history of modern biblical criticism happened in the seventeenth century. This time frame

14. Maddox, "Secular Reformation," 539-62; Geerken, "Machiavelli's Moses," 579-95; Marx, "Moses and Machiavellism," 551-71; Fubini, "Humanism and Truth," 79-86; Kugel, "Bible in the University," 143-65; Goshen-Gottstein, "Christianity," 69-88.

15. Frampton, *Spinoza and the Rise of Historical Criticism*, 23-42.

16. Morrow, *Three Skeptics and the Bible*, 139-48.

17. Cavanaugh, *Myth of Religious Violence*, 166-67.

18. Duffy, *Stripping of the Altars*, 377-523; Marx, *Faith in Nation*, 128-39, 153-61, 175-84.

marks a real shift, even though it built on trends, philosophies, and skillsets that predated this time. It was here where biblical interpretation began to be undertaken in purely philological or historical ways that were not intended to be pre-theological or even theological at all.[19] The figures I focused on in chapter two, as well as in *Three Skeptics and the Bible* and *Theology, Politics, and Exegesis*—namely, Isaac La Peyrère, Thomas Hobbes, Baruch Spinoza, and Richard Simon—were of particular importance in this context.[20] In supporting his employer the Prince of Condé's political aspirations of ousting King Louis XIV and becoming the first Protestant king of France, La Peyrère built upon the Renaissance tools of biblical criticism to deconstruct Scripture. He did this through utilizing the newest historical finds, hence sowing the seeds of doubt about biblical and ecclesiastical authority so as to reinterpret Scripture to suit his and the prince's own political machinations.[21] Thomas Hobbes, in his biblical criticism, attempted to support the status quo in post-Reformation England, where the state sovereign had absolute control over the spiritual and temporal realms within the land, including biblical interpretation, which was to be state-sponsored scholarship. Like La Peyrère, Hobbes used the newly-forming modern discipline of history in order to support his claims, likewise deconstructing the sacred text and naturalizing the supernatural in his biblical interpretations.[22]

Spinoza took both Hobbes's and La Peyrère's work further, laying the foundation for a more precise, ostensibly scientific method of biblical interpretation than had been developed thus far.[23] Simon followed the work of La Peyrère, Hobbes, and Spinoza, even as he attempted to distance himself from them. Unlike his three exegetical forbears, Simon attempted to defend Catholic tradition, but he did so by tearing apart the Bible, piece by piece, to emphasize that without Catholic tradition, all that remains is a bundle of contradictions. His prioritization of secular scholarship over Catholic orthodoxy, however, is demonstrated in his refusal to refrain from publication

---

19. Goshen-Gottstein, "Foundations of Biblical Philology," 77–94.
20. Goshen-Gottstein, "Textual Criticism," 376.
21. Parente, "Isaac de la Peyrère," 169–86; Quennehen, "L'auteur des *Préadamites*," 349–73; Popkin, "Millenarianism and Nationalism," 74–84.
22. Morrow, *Three Skeptics and the Bible*, 85–103; Coleman, "Thomas Hobbes," 642–69; Malherbe, "Hobbes et la Bible," 691–99; Pacchi, Hobbes e la filologia," 277–92.
23. Morrow, "Spinoza and the Theo–Political Implications," 374–87; Morrow, *Theology, Politics, and Exegesis*, 16–34; Morrow, *Three Skeptics and the Bible*, 104–38; Dungan, *History of the Synoptic Problem*, 198–260; Freedman, "Father of Modern Biblical Scholarship," 31–38.

even after his book was placed on the Index. His work became instrumental in early modern English and German biblical criticism, which furthered Spinoza's agenda into the eighteenth century.[24]

In the eighteenth century, several scholarly trends advanced the trajectory which had been set for modern biblical criticism in the seventeenth-century works of La Peyrère, Hobbes, Spinoza, and Simon. La Peyrère and Hobbes had attempted to deconstruct the biblical texts, but they lacked the necessarily philological skills and tools to make their project a success. Spinoza laid down a methodological framework that would be followed into the twenty-first century, and yet he never engaged sufficiently with the critical tools forged in the Renaissance, which many of his contemporaries in the seventeenth century were using. In Simon, we can see the Scripture begin to dissolve as a result of his more thorough incorporation of careful textual and philological analysis in addition to his linguistic abilities, which far surpassed those of La Peyrère and Hobbes. Although Simon used his methodological framework as an apologetic defense of Catholic tradition, in the eighteenth century, such methods began to erode Scripture even further, setting Spinoza's core hermeneutical method firmly in place, which was nothing other than the entrance of Cartesian skepticism into the realm of biblical criticism.

Although Spinoza's and Simon's works were both brought into the world of German scholarship in the eighteenth century, the most significant shift in biblical studies that occurred then was in the work of Johann David Michaelis. Michaelis was not intending to deconstruct the Bible; in fact, his work represents a very sophisticated attempt to defend traditional views concerning Scripture. In the realm of Pentateuchal source criticism, for example, he provided a scholarly response to Jean Astruc, who, building upon Simon's work, divided Genesis into various sources. Astruc wanted to defend traditional attributions of authorship against La Peyrère, Hobbes, Spinoza, and Simon, but Michaelis believed that Astruc conceded too much ground. Where Michaelis's significance lies, however, was in his nearly complete transition of the study of the Bible from the realm of theology to the realm of history and culture. Michaelis was a faithful biblical exegete, but, basing himself on the reigning German Classical scholarship

---

24. Morrow, *Theology, Politics, and Exegesis*, 35–51; Champion, "Père Richard Simon," 39–61; Woodbridge, "Richard Simon," 193–206; Reventlow, "Richard Simon," 11–36; Hazard, *La crise*, 125–36.

of the day, he attempted to create a neutral and objective philological approach to biblical interpretation.[25]

The important context here is Prussian nationalism and the rise of Enlightenment universities in the German-speaking world, such as the University of Göttingen and the University of Berlin. These university systems existed to make productive civil servants for the Germanic state.[26] The burgeoning fields of Classical studies and Pentateuchal source criticism influenced and shaped each other, as German scholars were attempting to cut their moorings from their Catholic past, with deep roots in Judaism and the Old Testament, and seek a home elsewhere, in ancient Rome and Greece. In so doing, they reconfigured their view of Christianity, not as flowing out of the Semitic ancient Near Eastern world, but as Indo-European at its core, which these scholars began to call Aryan.[27] Ancient Rome, Greece, and these scholars' own mythic pagan German past became the new virtuous model on which to build a prosperous future.

Such scholarship culminated in the studies of Julius Wellhausen in the period just before and after Bismarck's anti-Catholic *Kulturkampf*. Many of the moves made within biblical studies, which soon became viewed as unquestioned starting points, the assured results of "objective" scholarship, received their classical formulation in this period, in the wake of the First Vatican Council's definition of papal infallibility in 1870. Thus, they represent the response of increasingly anti-clerical states to the Catholic Church. Judaism was denigrated as a symbol of Catholicism, wherein Old Testament priesthood and modern Jewish traditions were viewed as representative of Catholic priests and Catholic traditions.[28]

---

25. Morrow, *Theology, Politics, and Exegesis*, 52–73; Legaspi, *Death of Scripture*, ix–xii, 27–51, 79–169 (on Michaelis) and 136–40 (on Astruc); Gibert, "De l'intuition," 174–89; Nahkola, "*Memoires* of Moses," 204–20; Sheehan, *Enlightenment Bible*, 103–4, 114–15, 126, 180, 184, 186–87, 190, 197, 210–15; Löwenbrück, "Johann David Michaelis," 113–28.

26. Legaspi, *Death of Scripture*, 27–51.

27. Legaspi, *Death of Scripture*, 53–77; Masuzawa, *Invention of World Religions*, xii–xiii, 24–26, 145–206; Vick, "Greek Origins," 483–500; Marchand, *Down from Olympus*.

28. Gross, *War Against Catholicism*; Farmer, "State *Interesse*," 15–49; Momigliano, "Religious History," 49–64.

The Politics of Modernism

As the twentieth century was beginning to approach its close, Edwin Yamauchi remarked: "Catholic scholars are now accepting interpretations that were earlier proposed by antisupernatural critics of Christianity."[29] What follows here is one narrative of how that occurred. As we have seen, Catholics have been involved in the development of modern biblical criticism at least as early as the medieval period, with Marsilius and Ockham. Such scholarship, however, has always remained on the fringe within the Catholic world, whereas it rapidly became dominant in the Protestant world.[30] It was the Modernists, during the Modernist crisis, who brought such modern biblical hermeneutics into the heart of Catholic scholarship.

The modern scholarly assumptions of Modernists like Loisy go back at least as far as Spinoza, and they pretended to be neutral and objective, that is, absent of prior commitments. This is not only false, but simply impossible. Such scholarship does not represent the absence of commitment but rather the relocation of it.[31] What such scholarship, devoid of traditional theological commitments, represented was state-sponsored biblical criticism.[32] Thus, when anti-clerical, violent revolutionaries utilized the works of Modernists like George Tyrrell, such use made sense in the broader theo-political context.[33] The theoretical anti-Catholicism implied in such works was now made explicit in violent political action, as had already occurred centuries earlier with the Protestant Reformation and its violent liquidation of the monasteries.

The political context within the century leading up to the Modernist crisis helps make the picture clearer. The early theological debate between throne and altar became a battle between the Church and ever more secular states in the modern period. States used their monopoly on coercive violence to remove church lands from the public sphere, exile religious orders, etc. Portugal, Spain, Naples, Sicily, and France banned the Jesuits and deported them to the Papal States. In 1773, these states forced Pope Clement

---

29. Yamauchi, "Episode of the Magi," 22.

30. See Kugel's comment: "It is no accident that, to this day, the great centers of modern biblical scholarship are to be found in largely Protestant countries—Germany and the Netherlands, Scandinavia and Great Britain, Canada and the United States" (Kugel, *How to Read the Bible*, 28–29).

31. Levenson, *Hebrew Bible*, 125.

32. Farmer, "State *Interesse*," 24.

33. Portier, *Divided Friends*, xix, 7–12; Misner, "Social Modernism," 18–35.

XIV to suppress the Jesuits, who were viewed as transnational since they circumvented the diocesan authority structures and were thus not under the direct control of state-appointed bishops.[34]

Within just over twenty years, Napoleon invaded the Papal States and compelled Pope Pius VI to agree to the Peace of Tolentino. On February 20, 1799, Napoleon's French soldiers captured Pius VI, who was deathly ill, and whisked him away to France where, six months later, he died as a prisoner. In 1801, Napoleon signed the Napoleonic Concordat with the Pope's successor, Pius VII. Based on this Concordat, Pius VII reconstituted the hierarchy according to Napoleon's desires and then crowned Napoleon emperor in France. After French troops occupied Rome, Napoleon asked Pius VII to give up his leadership of the Papal States. Pius VII refused, so Napoleon had his soldiers kidnap the Pope, who was only liberated when the Austrians forced Napoleon to abdicate his throne. Within his first three months back in Rome, Pius VII restored the Jesuits.

For the remainder of the nineteenth century, this political background leading up to the Modernist crisis was a concern for both the Magisterium as well as those espousing theological and philosophical views that would be condemned as Modernist. In response to these threats, Pope Gregory XVI asked Austria to invade and occupy the Papal States. With the succession of Pius IX to the papal throne, the Piedmontese revolutionaries asked the Pope to join their forces in ousting the Austrians, which the Pope refused. In response, they assassinated the prime minister of the Papal States while he was in parliament. France entered the fray after the Austrians fled in fear of the Piedmontese. Vatican I ended early, when the French left to fight the Prussians, leaving a vacuum in the Papal States that was filled by the Piedmontese, who wrested the region from the Catholic Church.[35] This anti-clerical and anti-Catholic hostile political climate of the nineteenth century was in a very real sense the start of what would become known as the Modernist crisis.

Some of the anti-Modernist measures taken to stomp out Modernism were overly harsh—in particular, the clandestine operations of the Sodalitium Pianum. Pope Benedict XV, himself once suspected of being a Modernist, along with Pope John XXIII, ultimately suppressed this organization.[36] Marvin O'Connell's description of the Sodalitium Pianum's

---

34. Duffy, *Saints & Sinners*, 193–94, 203–4; Portier, "Church Unity," 25–54.

35. Lease, "Vatican Foreign Policy," 31–55.

36. Portier, *Divided Friends*, 38–57; O'Connell, *Critics on Trial*, 321, 341, 348n68, 361–65; Poulat, *Intégrisme et Catholicisme*.

head, Umberto Benigni, as "sinister" and as "spy-master of a ragtag crew of informers and fanatics" is on target.[37] Their anonymous denouncements of Catholic professors, regardless of whether or not they were in fact Modernists, created a climate of hostility and even terror throughout Europe and the United States. Pope Benedict XVI's reflections on this time period show that he is deeply saddened by the ways in which his own professors were hurt during the conflict. When he was still Prefect for the Congregation of the Doctrine of the Faith, he wrote the following: "The danger of a narrow-minded and petty surveillance is no figment of the imagination, as the history of the Modernist controversy demonstrates."[38] Despite the unfair and at times unchristian response to supposed Modernism, however, the Church was undeniably threatened by Modernism.

The case of Loisy is particularly instructive since he was the paradigmatic Modernist. Loisy is the infamous Bible scholar who, in his *L'Évangile et l'Église* [*The Gospel and the Church*] quipped: "Jesus announced the Kingdom and what arrived was the Church."[39] Loisy's scholarship was not politically disinterested; in fact, political intrigue loomed large behind Loisy's work. While writing his *L'Évangile et l'Église*, Loisy was lobbying to become a bishop and the anti-Catholic Prince of Monaco was attempting to help get Loisy elected. The plan failed, but Loisy worked hard at rallying support for the position.[40]

Magisterial Teaching on Inspiration as a Response to Modernism

Long before Loisy was on the Vatican's radar, Pius IX called the First Vatican Council. The Council intended not only to resolve theological issues but also to resolve the political problems that were inextricable from such theological issues. The clearest example is the document *Pastor Aeternus* with its declarations on the authority of the papacy. The theological issue involved

---

37. O'Connell, *Critics on Trial*, 361. O'Connell writes further: "No one was safe. . . . The files of the sodality eventually bulged with the names of such alleged malefactors, whose guilt was maintained simply by the fact that they had been denounced" (O'Connell, *Critics on Trial*, 363).

38. Ratzinger, *Nature and Mission*, 66.

39. Loisy, *L'Évangile et l'Église*, 111.

40. Morrow, "Religion and Empire"; Hill, "Politics of Loisy's," 184–86; O'Connell, "Bishopric of Monaco," 26–51.

whether ultimate authority rested with a council of bishops or with the pope. The closely related political issue can be seen by the fact that the majority of the world's bishops were appointed by heads of state, and thus the call for a council of bishops to trump the pope was a thinly veiled mask to subjugate the Church to the concerns of modern European states.

When it comes to Magisterial teaching on Scripture, Modernists like Loisy were often in view, even though they went unnamed. Throughout most of the Church's history, Scripture's divine inspiration was assumed and clearly taught, but there were no systematic treatises on Scriptural inspiration. The *Catholic Bible Dictionary* is correct when it states that "the growing climate of intellectual skepticism" in the nineteenth century first caused "the doctrine of inspiration" to be "subjected to serious examination."[41] The first papal encyclical on Scripture was Pope Leo XIII's *Providentissimus Deus* in 1893.[42] In this foundational encyclical, Leo attempted to counter specific trends in biblical criticism like Loisy's. In the storm of the Modernist crisis, Pius X issued his 1907 apostolic letter, *Lamentabili Sane Exitu*, clarifying Catholic teaching on divine inspiration against Modernist attempts to limit inspiration. In several magisterial documents, the Church continued to develop, hone, and clarify its dogmatic teaching on the dual authorship of Scripture and the unique divine inspiration, which extends to every part of the Sacred Page: the Pontifical Biblical Commission's 1915 *Responsa*; Pope Benedict XV's 1920 encyclical *Spiritus Paraclitus*; and Venerable Pope Pius XII's 1943 encyclical *Divino Afflante Spiritu*. These clarifications culminated in the Second Vatican Council's Dogmatic Constitution on Divine Revelation, *Dei Verbum*. Ironically, the birth of the biblical question in the Modernist controversy is what necessitated the Church's clarification and detailed examination of the closely related questions of biblical interpretation and biblical inspiration.

The Current Crisis in Biblical Interpretation

The hermeneutical problems identified in the Modernist crisis are still with us. The abuses remain, as is evident in classrooms across the Catholic world. Unfortunately, the history has been misinterpreted, and these misinterpretations have become the standard revised histories through which important teachings, such as those contained in *Dei Verbum*, have been interpreted.

41. Hahn ed., *Catholic Bible Dictionary*, 383.
42. Arnold, "Lamentabili sane exitu," 24–51; Hill, "Leo XIII," 40.

Some trends within Catholic biblical scholarship have downplayed traditional patristic and medieval forms of exegesis, particularly typology, where Old Testament texts are read in light of their full flowering in the New Testament. The overwhelming majority of contemporary Catholic biblical interpretations in the academy virtually ignore magisterial teaching on Scripture's divine inspiration.[43] Since the focus of Catholic biblical scholarship leans heavily in the historical-critical direction, Scripture's human authorship tends to be the focus of such studies. But like its Modernist past, much of contemporary Catholic biblical scholarship implicitly calls into question magisterial teaching on the dual authorship of Scripture.

What has transpired is that the Catholic biblical scholarly guild has made the modern mythology of methodological neutrality to which the Modernists subscribed its own.[44] As with the modern academic discipline of history, modern Catholic biblical scholarship in general tends to operate under the false assumption that the methods used are comparable to the laboratory methodology of the hard sciences, like chemistry and physics.[45] *L'esprit géométrique* has won the day. Geometric reason and the discipline of mathematics, with its language of "proof," remains the paradigmatic example of rationality to many Bible scholars, Catholic or otherwise.

With the rise of postmodern—including feminist, postcolonial, and a host of other adjectives—thought, which is so widespread in all humanities disciplines, my critique of logical positivist thought, encyclopedic rationality, and, indeed, modern thought in general should ostensibly appear irrelevant. This problematic Modernism has been replaced, and the debates on that topic are now moot. Much of postmodernism, however, simply takes farther the very modern project it seeks to transcend. Postmodernity, with its Nietzschean genealogies and Derridean deconstructions, continues to perpetuate modern thought, even as it dissolves reigning ideologies in its relativistic acids.[46] Thus, although we can increasingly find feminist and other postmodern critiques of modern

---

43. On the Church's teaching on biblical inspiration, see Pitre, "Mystery of God's Word," 47–66; Gadenz, "Magisterial Teaching," 67–91.

44. See Hill, "Henri Bergson," 120. He writes: "Loisy had insisted historical scholarship be free of theological or philosophical presuppositions and instead rely on those facts that historians could ascertain based on the available evidence. Philosophy and theology followed from history, in his view, not the reverse."

45. Fasolt, "History and Religion," 10–26; Fasolt, "Red Herrings," 17–26; Fasolt, *Limits of History*; Novick, *Noble Dream*.

46. Schindler, *Heart of the World*.

historical criticism, this often amounts to a form of Freudian patricide. These methods seek to counter the method upon which they are built and on which their dependence continues.

The scholarly folklore is most transparent in the retelling of the history of Catholic biblical scholarship. Here, the Modernists are the heroic Saints and the Magisterial authorities, like Pope St. Pius X, represent the gates of hell attempting to overcome the Church. Most of the actual historians of the Modernist controversy are very careful historians who have done extremely valuable and important work in helping to shed light on a number of contextual matters that are essential for gaining an understanding of the events that transpired. And yet, even among such historians, we find gross exaggerations, demonstrating that a prejudicial treatment of the history is influencing its telling—for example, the comment that Alfred Loisy was "among Roman Catholic biblical scholars, the only one of outstanding distinction."[47]

Pope Benedict XVI has been one of the most significant voices in this discussion. In his programmatic 1989 essay on "Biblical Interpretation in Conflict," he pointed out the dangers of failure to recognize and critique the philosophical positions giving life to various biblical hermeneutics. Modern biblical criticism styles itself on the hard sciences, with a façade of neutrality and objectivity, but, as Pope Benedict points out, even the hard sciences—as the Heisenberg Principle demonstrates—are bereft of a purely neutral objectivity. And yet, we cannot simply return to pre-modern biblical interpretation, as if the historical critical method was never created, nor can we turn a blind eye to our rich heritage from the Saints of the past. Rather, what we need to do is use the best of both traditional biblical exegetical traditions and of modern historical interpretation.[48] The guide to any such *resourcement* has to be the Church's tradition and Magisterium so that the Bible is studied and read from the heart of the Church. This requires not only a hermeneutic of faith—as opposed to the Cartesian hermeneutic of skepticism, which lies at the heart of modern biblical criticism—but also a hermeneutic of continuity. Pope Benedict XVI has shown us what this looks like in his seminal work, *Jesus of Nazareth*.[49]

---

47. Barmann, "Pope and the English Modernists," 40.

48. Stallsworth, "Story of an Encounter," 107–8; Ratzinger, "Biblical Interpretation in Conflict," 91–126.

49. Benedict XVI, *Jesus of Nazareth I*.

The Mystery of Dual Authorship[50]

One of the fears modern Catholic Bible scholars apparently have is the eclipse of historical biblical interpretation. The Magisterium has again and again stressed the importance of the literal sense of Scripture, of reading the Bible within its proper historical context. There should be no talk of the death of the historical critical method if by such method a scholarly historical study of Scripture is meant. At their best, however, these methods are pre-theological and have very firm limits in what they can actually teach us. Too often, contemporary exegetes make claims which far outreach the capabilities of the methods they employ.

What needs to return to Catholic biblical scholarship is something that was prominent in the work of Catholic exegetes prior to the Modernist crisis, namely, the firm conviction that reason must be purified by faith. In the words of *Dei Filius*, from the First Vatican Council: "Faith is above reason." There are several explanations for this. One is that "faith delivers reason from errors and protects it and furnishes it with knowledge of many kinds." But ultimately, as *Dei Filius* makes clear, "reason is never rendered capable of penetrating these mysteries in the way in which it penetrates those truths which form its proper object. For the divine mysteries, by their very nature, so far surpass the created understanding."[51]

Historical criticism is certainly indispensable, but it is not more indispensable than the Catholic doctrine of the divine inspiration of Sacred Scripture. If anything, the mystery of the dual authorship of Scripture is more important than historical criticism or any modern form of exegesis. Negatively, this is because of historical criticism's limits, but positively, it is also because of the implications of divine inspiration. Historical criticism by definition cannot demonstrate the mysteries of faith, and those sacred mysteries are of the utmost importance for Catholic biblical interpretation. Furthermore, the Church's teaching concerning the divine inspiration of Sacred Scripture calls for an interpretation that does not exclusively rely on historical criticism. The Church's teaching that God is the primary author of Scripture imposes a hermeneutic of faith and of continuity on the biblical exegete.[52]

50. Hahn ed., *Catholic Bible Dictionary*, 384.

51. *Dei Filius* chapter 4 in Tanner, *Decrees*, 808.

52. For a programmatic discussion of what such a biblical interpretation can look like, see Hahn, *Covenant and Communion*; Hahn, "Worship in the Word," 101–36; Hahn, *Letter and Spirit*.

In this chapter, we have taken a look at the roots of the Modernist crisis in the Catholic Church at the end of the nineteenth century and at the dawn of the twentieth century. I argued that at its heart, the Modernist controversy was not only fundamentally about the biblical question but also gave birth to the biblical question in the Catholic world. Moreover, the issues involved in early twentieth-century Modernism have not left us; rather, they remain in the contemporary debate over the future of Catholic biblical scholarship. It has been my goal to emphasize how the Church's teaching on the divine inspiration of Scripture demands a hermeneutic of faith and of continuity. Only such a hermeneutic, which relies upon both the best current methods of interpretation as well as the best of the past, engaged in from the heart of the Church, can move us forward, positively, in reading and living the Scriptures as Catholics. All Catholic biblical exegesis should be oriented toward mystagogical exegesis; exegesis which draws us into participation in the divine liturgy where we become divinized. That is the ultimate goal of reading and studying Scripture.

5

Secularization and the Elusive Quest for Objective Biblical Interpretation

THE ACADEMIC STUDY OF religion and modern biblical studies in the university share a common origin—namely, the purported quest for objectivity. Both scholarly disciplines came of age in the nineteenth century, especially in German universities. Thus, it should come as no surprise that two of the most common designations for the academic study of religion in the university are German in origin: *Religionsgeschichte* and *Religionswissenschaft*. Throughout the present chapter, I use several phrases to describe the same disciplines. Thus, "the academic study of religion," "*Religionsgeschichte*," "*Religionswissenschaft*," "religious studies," and "comparative religion" are used interchangeably to describe the phenomenological approach to studying world religions in nineteenth, twentieth, and twenty-first century Western universities.

This chapter uses the terms "modern biblical studies," "biblical studies," "modern biblical criticism," "biblical criticism," and "historical criticism" interchangeably for roughly the same enterprise. Some who want to claim pronounced differences and distinguish later criticism from its foundations may find this problematic. My use of these terms as interchangeable stems from two related points. First, nascent historical criticism emerged in the early modern period as the first method that is recognizable as modern biblical studies and yet is distinct from what came before the modern period. Thus, although biblical philology and textual analysis—both of which are included in modern biblical studies—existed, arguably, from at least the patristic period, what emerged in the seventeenth century as historical criticism, perhaps in inchoate form, represented something new.[1]

---

1. Goshen-Gottstein, "Textual Criticism," 376.

Biblical philology, particularly a concern for developing a command of the original languages, existed in the patristic era, and there are a number of examples like Jerome.[2] Clearly, a fully-formed textual criticism would have to wait until the Renaissance, Reformation, or perhaps the modern period, but patristic authors like Augustine were already aware of different textual traditions and provided an account for them—in the case of Augustine, who was limited to reading the Bible in Latin, he had access to different textual traditions via the Latin Vulgate and the Vetus Latina.[3] Jerome himself engaged in a more thorough textual criticism.[4]

Secondly, historical criticism's continued hegemonic status in the academy also leads me to use it interchangeably with the other phrases denoting modern biblical studies in this present study. Although postmodern, feminist, liberation, canonical, narrative, overtly theological, and other methods are evidenced in scholarly journals and introductory textbooks, a survey of recent scholarly literature shows how indebted to historical critical methodologies the discipline remains.[5] More often than not, even the articles using other methodologies (e.g., source criticism, form criticism, and redaction criticism) assume and utilize historical critical methodologies.

For the purposes of this chapter, I will assume the history of the discipline of comparative religion along the lines Tomoko Masuzawa argues persuasively in her groundbreaking work *The Invention of World Religions*. Masuzawa identified the emergence of scholarly discourse on world religions as inseparable from European colonialism, and thus I will not spend time reviewing that history.[6] What this chapter accomplishes is a genealogical account of the advent of modern biblical criticism underscoring the secularizing framework within which the field operates. Historically, this secularizing trend had both theological and political aspects. The argument I make consists of three parts. In the first, I discuss

---

2. See Williams, "Lessons from Jerome's," 78.

3. Legaspi, "Unless You Believe"; Tabet Balady, "La hermenéutica bíblica," 181–93.

4. Williams, "Lessons from Jerome's," 79.

5. As the articles in any recent copy of the standard refereed journals in the field, e.g., *Journal of Biblical Literature*, *Zeitschrift für die alttestamentliche Wissenschaft*, *Zeitschrift für die neutestamentliche Wissenschaft*, *Vetus Testamentum*, *Novum Testamentum*, *Biblica*, *New Testament Studies*, *Catholic Biblical Quarterly*, *Journal for the Study of the Old Testament*, *Journal for the Study of the New Testament*, and the *Scandinavian Journal of the Old Testament* make clear.

6. Masuzawa, *Invention of World Religions*.

the theologies and politics which shaped the modern project, commenting on the link to the emergence of modern centralized European states. As Talal Asad informs us:

> Modernity is a *project*—or rather, a series of interlinked projects—that certain people in power seek to achieve. The project aims at institutionalizing a number of (sometimes, conflicting, often evolving) principles: constitutionalism, moral autonomy, democracy, human rights, civil equality, industry, consumerism, freedom of the market—and secularism. It employs proliferating technologies (of production, warfare, travel, entertainment, medicine) that generate new experiences of space and time, of cruelty and health, of consumption and knowledge. The notion that these experiences constitute "disenchantment"—implying a direct access to reality, a stripping away of myth, magic, and the sacred—is a salient feature of the modern epoch[7]

The second portion of this chapter describes the early history of the drive toward modern biblical criticism from the medieval through the early modern period. In the final section, I emphasize how the attempt to achieve objectivity continued in Enlightenment universities and in nineteenth-century academic contexts, which were often inseparable from European colonialism. Biblical criticism in the nineteenth century became, in William Farmer's words, "state supported biblical scholarship."[8]

Questioning Secularization

Before plunging into the genealogical history of modern biblical studies, it would be beneficial to review the development of modern notions of the religious and the secular, which undergird both religious studies and biblical studies in the academy today.[9] Asad, Paul Griffiths, and William

---

[7]. Asad, *Formations of the Secular*, 13. Writing further, Asad explains: "Modern projects do not hang together as an integrated totality, but they account for distinctive sensibilities, aesthetics, moralities. . . . What is distinctive about modernity *as a historical epoch* includes modernity as a political-economic project" (Asad, *Formations of the Secular*, 14).

[8]. Farmer, "State *Interesse*," 24.

[9]. A number of very useful histories of modern biblical scholarship exist. Some of the more important, in my mind, are Cameron ed., *New Cambridge History*; Hahn and Wiker, *Politicizing the Bible*; Gibert, *L'invention critique*; Sæbø ed., *Hebrew Bible/Old Testament II*; Reventlow, *Epochen der Bibelauslegung IV*; Reventlow, *Bibelautorität*; Kraus, *Geschichte der historisch-kritischen*.

Cavanaugh provide important discussions of this development, and I am relying on their foundational studies here.[10]

Emergence of Secular and Religious

In 1990, John Milbank famously quipped, "Once, there was no 'secular.'"[11] As any thorough study of antiquity demonstrates, Milbank's assertion is obvious when we take modern notions of what it means to be "secular" as our starting point. The broader context for this pithy phrase is:

> Once, there was no "secular." And the secular was not latent, waiting to fill more space with the steam of the "purely human," when the pressure of the sacred was relaxed. Instead there was the single community of Christendom, with its dual aspects of *sacerdotium* and *regnum*. The *saeculum*, in the medieval era, was not a space, a domain, but a time—the interval between fall and *eschaton*—where coercive justice, private property, and impaired natural reason must make shift to cope with the unredeemed effects of sinful humanity.[12]

In English, secularization entered the language with the violent dissolution of the monasteries in the English Reformation. Agents on behalf of the English crown forcibly removed or exterminated Catholics from land the Catholic Church owned, and such land—ostensibly taken in order to support England's peasants—was handed over to the crown's supporters among wealthy noble families.[13] Secular eventually became associated with the space absent of what we might call religious particularity. Once atheism, agnosticism, the New Age movement, and other, more amorphous spiritualities became prominent, God became one more example of religious particularity. Thus, secular—both then and now—tends to exclude God in the popular discourse.[14]

Prior to its emergence in the English language, the secular (*saeculum*) pertained to a sphere in time, in the world, which was saturated with

---

10. Cavanaugh, *Myth of Religious Violence*; Griffiths, *Problem of Religious*; Cavanaugh, "Fire Strong Enough," 397–420; Asad, *Genealogies of Religion*.

11. Milbank, *Theology and Social Theory*, 9.

12. Milbank, *Theology and Social Theory*, 9.

13. Morrow, *Three Skeptics and the Bible*, 10–53; Marx, *Faith in Nation*, e.g., 128–39, 153–61, 175–84; Duffy, *Stripping of the Altars*, 383–85, 397, 402–3, 462.

14. Rocha and Morrow, "Dancing on the Wall," 129–54.

God. In time, *saeculum* denoted linear history, which was created by God and which would come to an end when God brought it to an end.[15] As pertaining to the world, *saeculum* places an emphasis on the natural order and continues, for example, to play a significant role in official Catholic theology. In its dogmatic constitution on the church, *Lumen Gentium*, the Second Vatican Council taught that:

> The laity have their own special character which is secular [*saecularis*]. ... It is the special vocation of the laity to seek the kingdom of God by engaging in temporal affairs and ordering these in accordance with the will of God. They live in the world [*saeculo*], that is to say, in each and all of the world's occupations and affairs, and in the ordinary circumstances of family and social life; these are the things that form the context of their life. And it is here that God calls them to work for the sanctification of the world as it were from the inside, like leaven, through carrying out their own task in the spirit of the gospel.[16]

Similarly, Pope St. John Paul II wrote: "There are two areas in which lay people live their vocations. The first, and the best one suited to their lay state, is the secular world, which they are called to shape according to God's will."[17]

---

15. Rocha and Morrow, "Dancing on the Wall," 145; Milbank, *Theology and Social Theory*, 9.

16. *Lumen Gentium* 31 in Tanner, *Decrees*, 875. All quotations from the Second Vatican Council in this chapter are taken from Tanner, *Decrees*. Compare this with the comments in the Second Vatican Council's decree on the apostolate of the laity, *Apostolicam Actuositatem* §2: "Laypeople, sharing in the priestly, prophetic and kingly offices of Christ, play their part in the mission of the whole people of God in the church and in the world. They truly exercise their apostolate by labours for evangelising and sanctifying people, and by permeating the temporal order with the spirit of the gospel and so perfecting it. ... Since it is proper to the lay state to live in the midst of the world engaged in secular [*saecularium*] affairs, laypeople are called by God, with lives made fervent in the Christian spirit, to exercise their apostolate as leaven in the world" (Tanner, *Decrees*, 982).

17. John Paul II, *Ecclesia in America*. These thoughts dovetail with the ideas of Josemaría Escrivá, whom Pope John Paul II canonized in 2002. In one of Escrivá's most famous homilies, "Amar al mundo apasionadamente" (1967), we read: "God is calling you to serve him *in and from* civil, material, secular doings of human life: in a laboratory, in the hospital operating room, in the barracks, in the university chair, in the factory, in the workshop, in the field, in the home and in all the immense panorama of work, God awaits us each day. ... There is *something* holy, divine, hidden in the most common situations, that is up to each one of you to discover" (Escrivá, "Amar al mundo," 487).

The religious shares a developmental history with the secular. Religion nowadays tends to be understood as a general category with diverse instantiations, but in all cases, it is with limits; today, religion is regarded as a separate or distinct part of someone's life. In the past, however, Jews, Christians, and Muslims (for example) lived life in an attempt to follow God in all areas and aspects of their lives. Even if individuals did not live up to specific expectations in this regard, it would have been quite natural to make reference to God, norms pertaining to God, etc. In the modern period, in contrast, God and religion newly redefined has been expected to play a role only in certain, narrowly defined contexts, which tend to be private. When such religion enters the public realm, it does so only by way of trespassing. Evelyn Waugh captures this attitude marvelously in his famous novel *Brideshead Revisited*, particularly in a conversation between one of the primary protagonists, Charles, the erstwhile agnostic Anglican, and Brideshead, the Catholic firstborn son of the Marchmain family:

> [Charles]: "'For God's sake,' I said, for I was near to tears that morning, 'Why bring God into everything?'
>
> [Brideshead]: 'I'm sorry. I forgot. But you know that's an extremely funny question.'
>
> [Charles]: 'Is it?'
>
> [Brideshead]: 'To me. Not to you.'[18]

To Charles, the agnostic, emblematic of the modern individual, God does not belong in "everything," but members of the Catholic Marchmain family seem to "bring God into everything" unnaturally. In the modern period, Judaism, Christianity, and Islam join each other—and a host of other diverse traditions—as fellow members in the new category of "world religions," each relegated to the private sphere.[19]

For Augustine, religion had to do with worship; religion was the praise and worship justly rendered to God. As Cavanaugh underscores, "For Augustine... *religio* is not contrasted with some sort of secular realm of activity.

---

18. Waugh, *Brideshead*, 145. A similar conversation occurs earlier between Cordelia and Charles: "When we were alone she [Cordelia] said: 'Are you really an agnostic?' [Charles]: 'Does your family always talk about religion all the time?' [Cordelia]: 'Not all the time. It's a subject that just comes up naturally, doesn't it?' [Charles]: 'Does it? It never has with me before'" (Waugh, *Brideshead*, 93).

19. Masuzawa, *Invention of World Religions*, xi–xiii, 1–21, 107–20, 179–206; Griffiths, *Problems of Religious*, 1–12.

Any human pursuit can have its own (false) type of *religio*, its own type of idolatry: the worship of human works, land, etc. These, not something like 'paganism' or 'Judaism,' are contrasted to true worship."[20] In the Medieval period, Thomas Aquinas understood religion in this earlier sense of worship or piety, and to this end, he treated it as a species of justice, since religion thus understood was the authentic worship of God which justice required. Aquinas also used religion in the standard medieval and modern sense as pertaining to specific Catholic religious orders. In this period, religion referred to worship due to God, monastic discipline, or specific orders within the Catholic Church. In the early modern period, religion was redefined to denote a discreet phenomenological category pertaining to sets of beliefs or practices by which such communities and community members may be studied and colonized.[21] This transformation served the political aims of emerging modern centralized states in their attempts to domesticate specific traditions, especially Catholicism and Calvinism.[22]

The Theological Politics Enmeshed in Modern Secularization

Until relatively recently, secularization was often seen as a trademark of modernity, and if perhaps politically motivated, it was at least bereft of any theological influences. A growing number of scholars, however, have demonstrated the deep theological influences on the emergence of modernity.[23] Although some of these scholars see this as proof that modernity does not in fact have secular roots, a closer investigation reveals that the theological origins of modernity contain within them specific theologies which are secularizing by their very nature. This is specifically the case with their

---

20. Cavanaugh, *Myth of Religious Violence*, 63.

21. Augustine, *Augustine*, 225–31; Morrow, *Three Skeptics and the Bible*, 139–48; Aquinas, *Summa Theologiae*, II.II.81; Cavanaugh, *Myth of Religious Violence*, 57–122; Griffiths, *Problems of Religious*, 1–12; Cavanaugh, "Fire Strong Enough," 403–8; Asad, *Genealogies of Religion*, 27–54. In his *City of God*, Augustine later brings up difficulties and inadequacies with the phrase religion as pertaining to worship, mentioning that it typically pertains to human relationships (See Augustine, *City of God*, X.I.).

22. Morrow, *Three Skeptics and the Bible*, 139–48; Cavanaugh, *Myth of Religious Violence*, 123–80; Pickstock, *After Writing*, 146–54; Cavanaugh, "Fire Strong Enough," 398–403.

23. Nelson, *Hebrew Republic*; Gillespie, *Theological Origins*; Taylor, *Secular Age*.

privatization of religion, newly redefined.²⁴ Thus, Luther's concept of two kingdoms, although firmly set within his theological vision, in theory and in fact, it relegated spiritual matters to the private recesses of the individual's soul and left virtually all temporal matters in the hands of the state.²⁵

Gallicanism, Erastianism, and related Conciliarist movements are also representative of this trend.²⁶ They are certainly theological, but that does not mean they are bereft of a secularizing theology. It is important to move beyond the rigid dichotomization of secular and religious in the modern sense. Theology becomes secularizing, in the modern sense, when it banishes religion from the public sphere. When Church discipline loses its sting, Church membership becomes volunataristic, and ecclesiastical authority becomes merely suasive, a secularizing trend is at work, banishing God to some purely private sphere, in effect, if not also in theory. When we recognize in Gallicanism, etc., that the call for a council of primarily state-appointed national bishops to trump the transnational authority of the pope, we begin to unmask a thinly veiled secular political agenda, albeit one which is interwoven into the very fabric of these theological movements. In cases such as these, the roots of modernity are not merely theological but also secular and political.²⁷

Modern Biblical Criticism Emerges from within this Context

Modern biblical criticism shares its theological and political origins with modernity because it grew up within modernity as one of modernity's swords, serving in the combat that the modern project represents. In his groundbreaking article, "'A Fire Strong Enough to Consume the House': The Wars of Religion and the Rise of the State," Cavanaugh provides a genealogical account of the rise of modern centralized European states—which are

---

24. Cavanaugh, *Myth of Religious Violence*, 123–80; Cavanaugh, "Fire Strong Enough," 397–420.

25. Luther, "Von weltlicher Obrigkeit," 246–80. See the comments in Cavanaugh, "Fire Strong Enough," 399.

26. I recognize that especially French Gallicanism is incredibly diverse. See Congar, "Gallicanisme," 1731–39. Congar's entry may be old, but it remains, in my opinion, one of the finest treatments of Gallicanism.

27. Morrow, *Three Skeptics and the Bible*, 10–53; Portier, "Church Unity," 27–37.

the faces and engines of modernity.[28] Cavanaugh details how state centralization predated the early modern era by centuries, which, in other works, he maintains go back perhaps as far as the twelfth century, if not earlier.[29] As with Cavanaugh's arguments concerning the emergence of modern states, modern biblical criticism likewise did not appear *ex nihilo* from the minds of nineteenth-century savants but rather has deep roots in the medieval period. Such precursors develop in such a way that by the modern period, biblical criticism became, in Jon Levenson's words: "The realization of the Enlightenment project in the realm of biblical scholarship."[30]

Some Important Precursors Reviewed

Prior to the modern period and the development of what Michael Legaspi calls "the academic Bible"—that is, the Bible as a book to be studied by scholars in the university—there was "the scriptural Bible"—that is, the living Scriptures that Jews and Christians encountered, especially within their respective liturgies, interpreted by a panoply of exegetical traditions.[31] Traditional Jewish and Christian biblical interpretation was an immensely complex practice. For both Jews and Christians, the Scriptures themselves were difficult to understand and required serious effort. Because the Scriptures were meant for the faithful, this intellectual exertion was deemed worthwhile and indeed necessary.[32] In some ways, encountering Scripture was about encountering God; it was a means of "seeking the face of God" in this life.[33] Although most Jews and Christians were not primarily readers

---

28. Cavanaugh, "Fire Strong Enough," 397–420.

29. Cavanaugh, "Killing for the Telephone Company," 246–48. Regarding state centralization's early origins in the medieval period, Cavanaugh follows the arguments made in Strayer, *On the Medieval Origins*. See Jones, *Before Church and State* for a very important corrective to this history.

30. Levenson, *Hebrew Bible*, 118.

31. Legaspi, *Death of Scripture*, viii. For the contrast between these two Bibles and the origins of the academic Bible, see Legaspi, *Death of Scripture*, vii–x, 3–26. See also Morrow, *Three Skeptics and the Bible*, 139–48.

32. Kugel, *How to Read the Bible*, 10–24.

33. Here I am borrowing from the subtitle of Wilken, *Spirit of Early Christian*. Wilken explains his subtitle as follows: "The subtitle *Seeking the Face of God* is based on Psalm 105:4 in the Latin version, 'Seek his face always' (Quaerite faciem eius semper).... More than any other passage in the Bible, it captures the spirit of early Christian thinking" (Wilken, *Spirit of Early Christian*, xxii). In his third chapter, devoted to early Christian biblical interpretation and entitled, "The Face of God for Now," Wilken opens with a

of Scripture but hearers of Scripture, they listened attentively and actively in order to, as it were, seek the face of God here and now in the *saeculo*.[34] Christian interpretation relied upon multiple senses of Scripture. By the time of Augustine—who relied upon the *Rule* of the Donatist Tyconius—the *quadruplex sensus* became the standard interpretive form, with the two senses (literal and spiritual) and three spiritual senses (typological, tropological, anagogical).[35] Aquinas relied upon this hermeneutical framework in his own work when he taught about biblical interpretation.[36] Jewish interpretation was likewise as diverse as Christian.[37]

Already by the Medieval period, these traditional, multiple senses of Scripture began to erode with an emphasis on the literal sense, which triumphed in the Protestant Reformation. Of course, it is more accurate to say that the major Reformers broadened the *sensus literalis* rather than abandoned the traditional senses of Scripture, as their works include exegesis traditionally identified as typological and tropological.[38] To be quite fair, however, this expansion of the literal sense already began in the late medieval period.[39] As Deeana Klepper explains: "Sixteenth-century exegetes were able to abandon the fourfold sense of Scripture in favor of a 'purely' literal sense to whatever degree they did, largely because the innovations of

---

quotation from Augustine: "For now, treat the Scripture of God as the face of God. Melt in its presence" (Wilken, *Spirit of Early Christian*, 50).

34. Morrow, *Three Skeptics and the Bible*, 139–48; Candler, *Theology, Rhetoric, Manuduction*, 7, 9, 15, 18, 27, 38–39, 50, 66, 74, 77–82, 151–60, 162; van der Coelen, "Pictures for the People," 185–205; Wilken, *Spirit of Early Christian*, xiii–xxii, 25–79; Asad, *Formations of the Secular*, 37–38.

35. Morrow, "*Dei verbum*," 230–34; Synan, "Four 'Senses,'" 225–36; Minnis, "*Quadruplex Sensus*," 231–56; Simonetti, "L'ermeneutica biblica," 393–418; Tilley, "Understanding Augustine," 405–408; Freeman, "Figure and History," 319–29; Dulaey, "La sixième Règle," 83–103; Tilley, "Use of Scripture"; Bright, *Book of Rules*; Gaeta, "Le Regole," 109–18; Mayer, "Prinzipien der Hermeneutik," 197–211; and de Lubac, *Exégèse médiévale*. I am aware that exegesis within the ancient and medieval Christian world often went beyond the bounds of the *quadruplex sensus*, as pointed out in Bucur, "Sinai, Zion, and Tabor," 33–52; Bucur, "Exegesis of Biblical," 92–112. I am also aware of the problems with de Lubac's study, as pointed out ably by McDermott, "Henri de Lubac's Genealogy," 124–56.

36. Aquinas, *Summa Theologiae*, I., Q.1, A.10.

37. Kasher, "Interpretation of Scripture," 547–94; Walfish, "Introduction to Medieval," 3–12; Fishbane, "Midrash," 549–63; Talmage, "Apples of Gold," 313–55; Idel, "Midrashic Versus," 45–58.

38. See Steinmetz, "John Calvin," 282–91; Muller, "Hermeneutic of Promise," 68–82; Steinmetz, *Luther in Context*.

39. Klepper, "Theories of Interpretation," 427–38.

the thirteenth century had provided a model for incorporating figurative language and prophecy within the literal sense."[40]

During the same period, the specialist very rapidly began to take precedence over traditional ecclesial authorities.[41] Although precursors exist in people like Peter Abelard, who was likely influenced by Medieval Muslim commentators, mediated to him via Peter the Venerable, we find the clearest of precursors in Marsilius of Padua and William of Ockham.[42] The Protestant Reformers continued this trend, especially in their continuation of the humanistic preoccupation with the Bible's textual tradition and with their mastery of philology.[43]

Quests for Peace through Objectivity

It was in the seventeenth century that an ostensibly objective, departicularized biblical hermeneutic began to be sought, free of prior commitments. Although he had important precursors, Baruch Spinoza is one of the most central figures within this history.[44] Spinoza sought an objective scientific method for reading the Bible patterned on geometry and the emerging natural sciences. The primary motive put forward for Spinoza's work, as well as the prior work of his own disciple, Lodewijk Meyer, was to put an end to violent wars caused by religion, most notably the Thirty Years' War.

---

40. Klepper, "Theories of Interpretation," 437.

41. The politics of this shift in authority is often missed by scholars, but see the important insights in this regard in Fasolt, "Religious Authority," 364–80; Frampton, *Spinoza and the Rise of Historical Criticism*, 13.

42. See chapter four in this volume; Morrow, *Three Skeptics and the Bible*, 10–53; Minnis, "Material Swords," 292–308; Lazarus-Yafeh, *Intertwined Worlds*, 71–72; Arnaldez, *Grammaire et théologie*, 319; Asín Palacios, *Abenházam II*, 74, 74n105.

43. See chapter four in this volume; Morrow, *Three Skeptics and the Bible*, 10–53; Gibert, *L'invention critique*, 47–73; Waldstein, "Analogia Verbi," 100–1; Legaspi, *Death of Scripture*, 10–26; Frampton, *Spinoza and the Rise of Historical Criticism*, 23–42.

44. Several important precursors to Spinoza's work were actually among his contemporaries: Isaac La Peyrère, Thomas Hobbes, and Lodewijk Meyer. See chapters two and four of this present volume; Morrow, "Spinoza and the Theo-Political Implications," 374–87; Morrow, *Theology, Politics, and Exegesis*, 16–34; Morrow, *Three Skeptics and the Bible*, 10–148.

Colonial Pressures

The biblical critical work of the seventeenth century was received by eighteenth-century scholars in very different ways. Many scholars were uneasy with the skepticism of seventeenth-century biblical exegetes like Isaac La Peyrère and Spinoza, yet they assumed the basic methodological framework of scientific objectivity. The study of the Bible survived and thrived at Enlightenment universities because of such study's transformation from a theological discipline into an historical one. Biblical philology and history, once viewed as pre-theological enterprises, became independent and autonomous disciplines, and, in the Enlightenment university, they represented the only respectable approach to studying the Bible.[45]

Enlightenment Universities and the New Biblical Studies

Enlightenment universities in Germany were initially created to form good civil servants. This objective coincided with a focus on culture; the best citizens were those who were most loyal to the state. Thus, Legaspi writes:

> It was not at all clear that the study of the Bible in any form would have a place at a new university, especially one created by the government to educate civil servants and noblemen in the rational, tolerant spirit of the age. Yet, at Göttingen, academics succeeded in folding the humanities, though tied strongly to ancient texts and traditions, into a modern, statist enterprise.[46]

Likewise, in regard to the emphasis on culture (in the sense of both *Bildung* and also *Kultur*) and biblical scholarship, Jonathan Sheehan astutely notes: "Culture became a powerful tool in the rhetorical arsenal of German savants and would come to subsume man's entire spiritual, political, artistic, historical, and scholarly heritage."[47] Hence, German universities naturally sought to sever ties with Germany's Christian and especially Catholic past, which had the potential to undermine their goal, and they turned their attention to a search among non-Christian sources that contained excellent models of civic virtue. In time, the German quest came to be associated

---

45. Morrow, *Theology, Politics, and Exegesis*, 52–73; Legaspi, *Death of Scripture*, x–xi, 4–7, 9, 31–36, 81, 83–104, 155–59.

46. Legaspi, *Death of Scripture*, x.

47. Sheehan, *Enlightenment Bible*, 223.

with the search among ancient Rome, Greece, and pre-Christian Germanic history, in the hopes of uncovering the cultural past necessary to supplant Christianity and found a new Germany.[48]

Legaspi shows in his recent work, *The Death of Scripture and the Rise of Biblical Studies*, that the Bible became transformed from a theological wellspring into a cultural and historical artifact from a long dead civilization through the work of university professors, particularly Johann David Michaelis at the University of Göttingen.[49] The model for Michaelis's project was the German classicists Johann Matthias Gesner and Christian Gottlob Heyne's wholesale transformation of Classical studies. It would take Michaelis's disciple, Johann Gottfried Eichhorn, to tread where Michaelis dared not go, and dissolve Scripture into fragments by means of Eichhorn's acidic methodology.[50] Legaspi makes an important fundamental point when he writes:

> The two [the scriptural and academic Bibles] are opposed to one another, but I believe it is necessary to reconceive the nature of this opposition. Too often it has been seen, unhelpfully, as an expression of stale antitheses between reason and faith, history and revelation, the secular and the sacred. The history of modern biblical criticism shows that the fundamental antitheses were not intellectual or theological but rather social, moral, and political. Academic critics did not dispense with the authority of a Bible resonant with religion; they redeployed it.[51]

This is what happened in later centuries as they followed the work of their predecessors.

---

48. Morrow, *Theology, Politics, and Exegesis*, 52–73; Legaspi, *Death of Scripture*, especially x–xi, 27–78, 156–60, 164–66; Hauerwas, *State of the University*, 12–32; Sheehan, *Enlightenment Bible*, especially 211–17; D'Costa, *Theology in the Public Square*, 8–20; Williamson, *Longing for Myth*; Vick, "Greek Origins," 483–500; Marchand, *Down from Olympus*.

49. Morrow, *Theology, Politics, and Exegesis*, 52–73; Legaspi, *Death of Scripture*.

50. Legaspi, *Death of Scripture*, 128, 136, 156, 165; Gibert, *L'invention critique*, 305–6, 323–25, 327–30, 346; Sheehan, *Enlightenment Bible*, 90, 199, 214, 219–20. Legaspi explains: "In the main, the guiding light of our eighteenth-century figures was not a beautiful vision of what criticism as a theological enterprise might look like. It was rather, for them, a matter of what biblical criticism, as a university subject, might *do*, what it might contribute to the education of men who would one day run the governments under which they themselves would have to live" (Legaspi, *Death of Scripture*, 31).

51. Legaspi, *Death of Scripture*, xii.

The Fate of Academic Biblical Studies in the Twentieth and Early Twenty-First Century

Biblical studies in the university thus became a tool of statecraft. Ever more secular, biblical studies taught in classrooms and as practiced in scholarship attempted to departicularize the various religious and theological commitments of scholars. As Levenson explains: "Like citizens in the classical liberal state, scholars practicing historical criticism of the Bible are expected to eliminate or minimize their communal loyalties, to see them as legitimately operative only within associations that are private, nonscholarly, and altogether voluntary."[52] Under the guise of objectivity, scholars began pushing agendas which supported their political concerns.[53] In the nineteenth century, the brunt of the attack was against contemporary Judaism and Catholicism, the latter of which scholars like Julius Wellhausen saw as the bastard child of a long dead Judaism.[54] These biblical critical projects already became embroiled in European colonialism in the eighteenth century, but particularly, in the case of Germany, by the end of the nineteenth century and the early part of the twentieth century.[55]

To conclude, as with the academic study of religion, modern biblical studies emerged from the quest for objectivity in the attempt to create distance between the Bible and the scholar, suppressing all prior

---

52. Levenson, *Hebrew Bible*, 118. Writing further, he maintains: "The new arrangement... tends subtly to restrict the questions studied and the methods employed to those that permit the minimization of religious difference with relative facility.... Those unwilling to pay the price are unable to participate in this type of study" (Levenson, *Hebrew Bible*, 118).

53. Something similar occurred in the discipline of history as well. See Novick, *Noble Dream*.

54. See Gerdmar, *Roots of Theological*, 39–41, 54–57, 64–69, 77, 79, 82, 93, 115–17, 119–20, 588–89; Pasto, "W. M. L. de Wette," 33–52; Pasto, "Islam's 'Strange Secret Sharer,'" 437–74; Pasto, "When the End," 157–202; Manuel, *Broken Staff*, 311. On the political context, and especially the role of the *Kulturkampf* (as well as the history immediately preceding the *Kulturkampf*), within which it is necessary to place the works of scholars like Wellhausen, see Gross, *War Against Catholicism*; Farmer, "State *Interesse*," 15–49; Simon, "History As a Case-Study," 168–96; Momigliano, "Religious History," 49–64.

55. Already in the eighteenth century, "German intellectuals of the late Enlightenment were engaging in dialogue with the colonial restructuring of the world" (Noyes, "Goethe on Cosmopolitanism," 443). On the link between colonial enterprises and biblical studies during this time, see Legaspi, *Death of Scripture*, 95–97; Sheehan, *Enlightenment Bible*, especially 186–217; Arnold and Weisberg, "Delitzsch in Context," 37–45; Arnold and Weisberg, "Centennial Review," 441–57; Holloway, "Biblical Assyria," pars. 1–21; and Silberman, *Digging for God*.

commitments. A study of the history of such scholarship reveals the modern politics which undergirded the development of biblical criticism. In this history, the theological and the secular were not in dire combat, so much as certain theological politics were at odds with one another. The colonial projects of modern European states, especially Germany, gave shape and texture to the discipline, as it spread from German universities to the English speaking world and beyond. This is an interesting reversal, since Germany was actually a late-comer to the game of modern biblical criticism, initially building upon the work of English Deists and rationalists in biblical criticism, Germany eventually became master of the field and then later influenced the very England on whose own foundational studies it had built.[56] As Sheehan comments:

> The Enlightenment Bible was delivered in Germany by those committed to transforming, not preserving, the *textus receptus*. ... This initial difference of position allowed the Enlightenment Bible to thrive in Germany, thrive to such an extent that the enormous outflow of intellectual energy from England to Germany in the early eighteenth century was, by century's end, completely reversed, as Germany became the center of a vibrant biblical scholarship, the envy of Protestant nations across Europe.[57]

As we are only too aware, the quixotic quest for objective neutrality has often resulted not in illumination but obfuscation. As Levenson explains: "The secularity of historical criticism represents not the suppression of commitment, but its relocation."[58]

---

56. See Gibert, *L'invention critique*, 309–16; Legaspi, *Death of Scripture*, 115–21; Sheehan, *Enlightenment Bible*, 27–30; Rogerson, *Old Testament Criticism*; Reventlow, *Bibelautorität*.

57. Sheehan, *Enlightenment Bible*, 30.

58. Levenson, *Hebrew Bible*, 125.

Conclusion

THE HISTORY OF MODERN biblical criticism begins before the modern period. It stretches back at least into the late medieval period in the fourteenth century. In the first chapter we took a more extensive look at the early history than I had in *Theology, Politics, and Exegesis*.[1] Taking Scott Hahn and Benjamin Wiker as our primary guides through this history,[2] I examined the philosophical and political contexts in which early modern biblical criticism began to develop in the fourteenth century and through the period commonly known as the Protestant Reformation. In the second chapter, I turned to look more carefully at the three pivotal seventeenth-century figures I had explored earlier in *Three Skeptics and the Bible*: Isaac La Peyrère,[3] Thomas Hobbes,[4] and Baruch Spinoza.[5] Although my prior treatment was more extensive, this chapter represents a great improvement of that work, based on further research to indicate how these three all had political motivations for their methods of biblical criticism.

The third chapter continued the history through the seventeenth and into the beginning of the eighteenth centuries, again expanding upon what I had touched upon only briefly in *Theology, Politics, and Exegesis*, concluding with the Deistic exegesis of John Toland and again taking Hahn and Wiker as our main guides.[6] The fourth chapter explored the history of Catholic notions of biblical inspiration as it related to the much broader history of biblical interpretation, from antiquity to the Roman Catholic

---

1. Morrow, *Theology, Politics, and Exegesis*, 2–8.
2. Hahn and Wiker, *Politicizing the Bible*.
3. Morrow, *Three Skeptics and the Bible*, 54–84.
4. Morrow, *Three Skeptics and the Bible*, 85–103.
5. Morrow, *Three Skeptics and the Bible*, 104–38.
6. Morrow, *Theology, Politics, and Exegesis*, 8–15; Hahn and Wiker, *Politicizing the Bible*.

modernist controversy at the dawn of the twentieth century. We saw how shifts in biblical interpretation sometimes translated into shifting notions of biblical inspiration and how the Magisterium responded to skeptical criticism by articulating its notion of inspiration.

The fifth chapter concluded this volume by exploring the quest for objectivity which lay at the heart of modern biblical criticism early on, and how this quest fits historically within the broader context of secularization. An important fruit of this study calls into question standard genealogies of modernity, the state, and even the secular. John Milbank was correct when he wrote, "Once, there was no secular"[7]—at least not in the modern sense. But we might add, inspired by Andrew Jones's recent work, "Once, there was no church and state"[8]—at least not in the modern sense (and political aspiration) of church and state, separable into neat and tidy, hermetically-sealed spheres of operation.

One lesson this history teaches is that there never has been a purely objective, formally neutral, completely disinterested approach to the biblical interpretation. Nor can there ever be, as Pope Benedict has highlighted.[9] But nor should we necessarily desire such disinterest. I am persuaded, as Benedict has argued, that, "only faith's hermeneutic is sufficient."[10] Why is this? One reason is because the lover knows the beloved far better and more authentically than the so-called objective, disinterested, observer. In the same way, we will understand Scripture better the more we fall in love with it, the more of a claim it wields on our lives. So in a sense, this is a call to grow old with Scripture, to grow old with the Sacred Page, with a love ever new. While more work of analysis for these early biblical critics may be helpful, there is also a need to move forward to a constructive biblical exegesis that benefits from the insights of modern biblical criticism without being beholden to the underlying political motivations that often resulted in false notions of fact and objectivity in the study of the Bible.

---

7. Milbank, *Theology and Social Theory*, 9.

8. Jones, *Before Church and State*. This is not a quotation but rather a play on Milbank's quotation in light of the point of Jones's book.

9. Ratzinger, "Biblical Interpretation in Conflict," 91–126.

10. Ratzinger, *Behold the Pierced One*, 45.

Bibliography

Abu Laila, Muhammad. "Ibn Ḥazm's Influence on Christian Thinking in Research." *Islamic Quarterly* 31 (1987) 103–15.
Åkerman, Susanna. *Queen Christina of Sweden and Her Circle: The Transformation of a Seventeenth-Century Philosophical Libertine*. Leiden: Brill, 1991.
Almond, Philip C. *Adam & Eve in Seventeenth-Century Thought*. Cambridge: Cambridge University Press, 1999.
Anderson, Gary A. *Charity: The Place of the Poor in the Biblical Tradition*. New Haven: Yale University Press, 2013.
———. "Redeem Your Sins by the Giving of Alms: Sin, Debt, and the 'Treasury of Merit' in Early Jewish and Christian Tradition." *Letter & Spirit* 3 (2007) 36–67.
Aquilina, Mike. *Good Pope, Bad Pope*. Cincinnati: Servant, 2013.
Aquinas, Thomas. *In psalmos Davidis expositio*. http://www.corpusthomisticum.org/iopera.html.
———. *Quaestiones disputatae de potentia*. http://www.corpusthomisticum.org/iopera.html.
———. *Summa Theologiae*. Cambridge: Blackfriars, 1964.
Arnaldez, Roger. *Grammaire et théologie chez Ibn Hazm de Cordoue: Essai sur la structure et les conditions de la pensée musulmane*. Paris: Librairie Philosophique J. Vrin, 1956.
———. "Spinoza et la pensée arabe." *Revue de Synthèse* 99 (1978) 151–74.
Arnold, Bill T., and David B. Weisberg. "A Centennial Review of Friedrich Delitzsch's 'Babel und Bibel' Lectures." *Journal of Biblical Literature* 121 (2002) 441–57.
———. "Delitzsch in Context." In *God's Word for Our World*, edited by J. Harold Ellens, et al., 37–45. Vol. 2. London: T&T Clark, 2004.
Arnold, Claus. "'Lamentabili sane exitu' (1907). Das Römische Lehramt und die Exegese Alfred Loisys." *Zeitschrift für neuere Theologiegeschichte/Journal for the History of Modern Theology* 11.1 (2004) 24–51.
Asad, Talal. *Formations of the Secular: Christianity, Islam, Modernity*. Stanford: Stanford University Press, 2003.
———. *Genealogies of Religion: Disciplines and Reasons of Power in Christianity and Islam*. Baltimore: Johns Hopkins University Press, 1993.
Ashcraft, Richard. *Revolutionary Politics & Locke's Two Treatises of Government*. Princeton: Princeton University Press, 1986.
Asín Palacios, Miguel. *Abenházam de Córdoba y su historia crítica de las ideas religiosas II*. Madrid: Tipografía de la "Revista de Archivos, Bibliotecas y Museos," 1928.
Augustine. *Augustine: Earlier Writings*. Philadelphia: Westminster, 1953.

———. *City of God*. New York: Penguin, 2003.
Auvray, Paul. "Richard Simon et Spinoza." In *Religion, érudition et critique à la fin du XVIIe siècle et au début du XVIIIe*, edited by Baudouin de Gaiffier, et al., 201–14. Paris: Presses universitaires de France, 1968.
Barmann, Lawrence. "The Pope and the English Modernists." *US Catholic Historian* 25.1 (2007) 31–54.
Barnouw, Jeffrey. "The Separation of Reason and Faith in Bacon and Hobbes, and Leibniz's Theodicy." *Journal of the History of Ideas* 42.4 (1981) 607–28.
Barthélemy, Dominique. *Studies in the Text of the Old Testament: An Introduction to the Hebrew Old Testament Text Project: English Translation of the Introductions to Volumes 1, 2, and 3 Critique textuelle de l'Ancien Testament*. Winona Lake: Eisenbrauns, 2012.
Baumgold, Deborah. "Hobbes's and Locke's Contract Theories: Political not Metaphysical." *Critical Review of International Social and Political Philosophy* 8.3 (2005) 289–308.
Benítez, Miguel. "La posterité de La Peyrère: *Dissertation sur l'origine des Négres & des Américains*." In *La geografia dei saperi: Scritti in memoria di Dino Pastine*, edited by Domenico Ferraro and Gianna Gigliotti, 183–202. Florence: La Lettere, 2000.
Berman, Joshua. "CTH 133 and the Hittite Provenance of Deuteronomy 13." *Journal of Biblical Literature* 130.1 (2011) 25–44.
Bernier, Jean. *La critique du Pentateuque de Hobbes à Calmet*. Paris: Honoré Champion, 2010.
Beyssade, Michelle. "Deux latinistes: Descartes et Spinoza." In *Spinoza to the Letter: Studies in Words, Texts and Books*, edited by Fokke Akkerman and Piet Steenbakkers, 55–68. Leiden: Brill, 2005.
Boyle, John F. "Authorial Intention and the *Divisio textus*." In *Reading John with St. Thomas Aquinas: Theological Exegesis and Speculative Theology*, edited by Michael Dauphinais and Matthew Levering, 3–8. Washington, DC: Catholic University of America Press, 2005.
Brecht, Martin. *Martin Luther: His Road to Reformation, 1483-1521*. Translated by J. Schaaf. Philadelphia: Fortress, 1985.
Bright, Pamela. *The Book of Rules of Tyconius: Its Purpose and Inner Logic*. Notre Dame: University of Notre Dame Press, 1988.
Bucur, Bogdan G. "Exegesis of Biblical Theophanies in Byzantine Hymnography: Rewritten Bible?" *Theological Studies* 68 (2007) 92–112.
———. "Sinai, Zion, and Tabor: An Entry into the Christian Bible." *Journal of Theological Interpretation* 4 (2010) 33–52.
Bunce, Robin. "Thomas Hobbes's Relationship with Francis Bacon—An Introduction." *Hobbes Studies* 16.1 (2003) 41–83.
Callaghan, G. K. "Nominalism, Abstraction, and Generality in Hobbes." *History of Philosophy Quarterly* 18.1 (2001) 37–55.
Calvert, Kenneth R. "Edwin M. Yamauchi." In *The Light of Discovery: Studies in Honor of Edwin M. Yamauchi*, edited by John D. Wineland, 1–23. Eugene, OR: Pickwick, 2007.
Cameron, Euan, ed. *The New Cambridge History of the Bible Volume 3: From 1450 to 1750*. Cambridge: Cambridge University Press, 2016.
Candler, Peter M. Jr. *Theology, Rhetoric, Manuduction, or Reading Scripture Together on the Path to God*. Grand Rapids: Eerdmans, 2006.
Cassuto, Umberto. *The Documentary Hypothesis and the Composition of the Pentateuch: Eight Lectures*. Translated by Israel Abrahams. Jerusalem: Shalem, 2006 (1941).
———. *La questione della Genesi*. Florence: Le Monnier, 1934.

Cavanaugh, William T. "'A Fire Strong Enough to Consume the House': The Wars of Religion and the Rise of the State." *Modern Theology* 11 (1995) 397–420.

———. "Killing for the Telephone Company: Why the Nation-State is Not the Keeper of the Common Good." *Modern Theology* 20.2 (2004) 243–74.

———. *The Myth of Religious Violence: Secular Ideology and the Roots of Modern Conflict.* Oxford: Oxford University Press, 2009.

Champion, Justin A. I. "Père Richard Simon and English Biblical Criticism, 1680–1700." In *Everything Connects: In Conference with Richard H. Popkin: Essays in His Honor*, edited by James E. Force and David S. Katz, 39–61. Leiden: Brill, 1999.

Coleman, Frank M. "Thomas Hobbes and the Hebraic Bible." *History of Political Thought* 25.4 (2004) 642–69.

Congar, Yves. "Gallicanisme." In *Catholicisme IV*, edited by G. Jacquemet, 1731–39. Paris: Letouzey et Ané, 1956.

Curley, Edwin. *Behind the Geometrical Method: A Reading of Spinoza's Ethics.* Princeton: Princeton University Press, 1988.

———. "Kissinger, Spinoza, and Genghis Khan." In *The Cambridge Companion to Spinoza*, edited by Don Garrett, 315–42. Cambridge: Cambridge University Press, 1996.

———. "Spinoza's Exchange with Albert Burgh." In *Spinoza's Theological-Political Treatise: A Critical Guide*, edited by Yitzhak Y. Melamed and Michael A. Rosenthal, 11–28. Cambridge: Cambridge University Press, 2010.

———. "Spinoza's Geometric Method." *Studia Spinozana* 2 (1986) 151–69.

D'Costa, Gavin. *Theology in the Public Square: Church, Academy, and Nation.* Oxford: Blackwell, 2005.

de Lubac, Henri. *Exégèse médiévale: les quatre sens de l'Ecriture.* 4 vols. Paris: Aubier-Montaigne, 1959, 1961, and 1964.

Djedi, Youcef. "Spinoza et l'islam: un état des lieux." *Philosophiques* 37 (2010) 275–98.

Donagan, Alan. *Spinoza.* Chicago: University of Chicago Press, 1989.

———. "Spinoza's Theology." In *The Cambridge Companion to Spinoza*, edited by Don Garrett, 343–82. Cambridge: Cambridge University Press, 1996.

Duffy, Eamon. *Saints & Sinners: A History of the Popes.* 3rd ed. New Haven: Yale University Press, 2006 (1997).

———. *The Stripping of the Altars: Traditional Religion in England 1400–1580.* New Haven: Yale University Press, 2005 (1992).

Dulaey, Martine. "La sixième Règle de Tyconius et son résumé dans le 'De doctrina christiana.'" *Revue des Études Augustiniennes* 35 (1989) 83–103.

Dungan, David Laird. *A History of the Synoptic Problem: The Canon, the Text, the Composition, and the Interpretation of the Gospels.* New Haven: Yale University Press, 1999.

Elazar, Daniel J. "Spinoza and the Bible." *Jewish Political Studies Review* 7 (1995) 5–19.

Escrivá, Josemaría. "Amar al mundo apasionadamente." In *Coversaciones con Mons. Escrivá de Balaguer: Edición crítico-histórica*, edited by José Luis Illanes and Alfredo Méndiz, 481–508. Madrid: Instituto Histórico San Josemaría Escrivá de Balaguer Ediciones Rialp, 2012.

Farmer, William R. "State *Interesse* and Markan Primacy: 1870–1914." In *Biblical Studies and the Shifting of Paradigms, 1850–1914*, edited by Henning Graf Reventlow and William Farmer, 15–49. Sheffield: Sheffield Academic, 1995.

BIBLIOGRAPHY

Fasolt, Constantin. "History and Religion in the Modern Age." *History and Theory* 45 (2006) 10–26.

———. *The Limits of History*. Chicago: University of Chicago Press, 2004.

———. "Red Herrings: Relativism, Objectivism, and Other False Dilemmas." *Storia della storiografia* 48 (2005) 17–26.

———. "Religious Authority and Ecclesiastical Governance." In *The Renaissance World*, edited by John Jeffries Martin, 364–80. London: Routledge, 2007.

Fishbane, Michael. "Midrash and the Meaning of Scripture." In *The Interpretation of the Bible: The International Symposium in Slovenia*, edited by Jože Krašovec, 549–63. Sheffield: Sheffield Academic, 1998.

Fraenkel, Carlos. "Reconsidering the Case of Elijah Delmedigo's Averroism and its Impact on Spinoza." In *Renaissance Averroism and its Aftermath: Arabic Philosophy in Early Modern Europe*, edited by Anna Akasoy and Guido Guiglioni, 213–36. Dordrecht: Springer, 2012.

———. "Spinoza on Philosophy and Religion: The Averroistic Sources." In *The Rationalists: Between Tradition and Innovation*, edited by Carlos Fraenkel et al., 58–81. Dordrecht: Springer, 2010.

Frampton, Travis L. *Spinoza and the Rise of Historical Criticism of the Bible*. London: T&T Clark, 2006.

Freedman, R. David. "The Father of Modern Biblical Scholarship." *Journal of the Ancient Near Eastern Society* 19 (1989) 31–38.

Freeman, Curtis W. "Figure and History: A Contemporary Reassessment of Augustine's Hermeneutic." In *Collectanea Augustiniana III: Augustine, Presbyter Factus Sum*, edited by Joseph T. Lienhard, et al., 319–29. New York: Peter Lang, 1993.

Freudenthal, Jakob. *Spinoza: Leben und Lehre*. Heidelberg: Carl Winter, 1927.

———. "Spinoza und die Scholastik." In *Philosophische Aufsätze. Eduard Zeller zu seinem fünfzigjährigen Doctor-Jubiläum gewidmet*, 84–138. Leipzig: Fues's Verlag, 1887.

Fubini, Riccardo. "Humanism and Truth: Valla Writes Against the Donation of Constantine." *Journal of the History of Ideas* 57 (1996) 79–86.

Gabbey, Alan. "Spinoza's Natural Science and Methodology." In *The Cambridge Companion to Spinoza*, edited by Don Garrett, 142–91. Cambridge: Cambridge University Press, 1996.

Gabriel, Frédéric. "Periegesis and Skepticism: La Peyrère, Geographer." In *Skepticism in the Modern Age: Building on the Work of Richard Popkin*, edited by José R. Maia Neto, et al., 159–70. Leiden: Brill, 2009.

Gadenz, Pablo T. "Magisterial Teaching on the Inspiration and Truth of Scripture: Precedents and Prospects." *Letter & Spirit* 6 (2010) 67–91.

Gaeta, Giancarlo. "Le *Regole* per l'interpretazione della Scrittura da Ticonio ad Agostino." *Annali di storia dell'esegesi* 4 (1987) 109–18.

Gallicet-Calvetti, Carla. "In margine a Spinoza lettore del *De cive* di Hobbes." *Rivista di filosofia neoscolastica* 73 (1981) 52–84, 235–63.

Garrido, Juan José. "El método histórico-crítico de interpretación de la Escritura según Spinoza." In *El método en teología. Actas del primer Simposio de Teología e Historia (29–31 mayo 1980)*, edited by the Faculty of Theology of Saint Vincent Ferrer, 269–81. Valencia: The Faculty of Theology of Saint Vincent Ferrer, 1981.

———. "La desmitificación de la Escritura en Spinoza." *Taula* 9 (1988) 3–45.

Geerken, John H. "Machiavelli's Moses and Renaissance Politics." *Journal of the History of Ideas* 60.4 (1999) 579–95.

Gerdmar, Anders. *Roots of Theological Anti-Semitism: German Biblical Interpretation and the Jews, from Herder and Semler to Kittel and Bultmann*. Leiden: Brill, 2008.

Gibert, Pierre. "De l'intuition à l'évidence: La multiplicité documentaire dans la Genèse chez H. B. Witter et Jean Astruc." In *Sacred Conjectures: The Context and Legacy of Robert Lowth and Jean Astruc*, edited by John Jarick, 174–89. London: T&T Clark, 2007.

———. *L'invention critique de la Bible: XVe–XVIIIe siècle*. Paris: Gallimard, 2010.

———. *L'invention de l'exégèse moderne: Les "Livres de Moïse" de 1650 à 1750*. Paris: Cerf, 2003.

Gillespie, Michael Allen. *The Theological Origins of Modernity*. Chicago: University of Chicago Press, 2008.

Gordon, Cyrus H. "Higher Critics and Forbidden Fruit." *Christianity Today* 4 (1959) 131–34.

———. *A Scholar's Odyssey*. Atlanta: Society of Biblical Literature, 2000.

Goshen-Gottstein, M. H. "Christianity, Judaism and Modern Bible Study." In *Congress Volume: Edinburgh 1974*, 69–88. Leiden: Brill, 1975.

———. "Foundations of Biblical Philology in the Seventeenth Century Christian and Jewish Dimensions." In *Jewish Thought in the Seventeenth Century*, edited by Isadore Twersky and Bernard Septimus, 77–94. Cambridge: Harvard University Press, 1987.

———. "The Textual Criticism of the Old Testament: Rise, Decline, Rebirth." *Journal of Biblical Literature* 102.3 (1983) 365–99.

Grafton, Anthony. *Joseph Scaliger: A Study in the History of Classical Scholarship I: Textual Criticism and Exegesis*. Oxford: Oxford University Press, 1983.

———. *Joseph Scaliger: A Study in the History of Classical Scholarship II: Historical Chronology*. Oxford: Oxford University Press, 1993.

Griffiths, Paul J. *Problem of Religious Diversity*. Oxford: Blackwell, 2001.

Gross, Michael B. *The War Against Catholicism: Liberalism and the Anti-Catholic Imagination in Nineteenth-Century Germany*. Ann Arbor: University of Michigan Press, 2004.

Gruntfest, Jacob. "Spinoza as a Linguist." *Israel Oriental Society* 9 (1979) 103–28.

Haarmann, Ulrich. "In Quest of the Spectacular: Noble and Learned Visitors to the Pyramids Around 1200 A.D." In *Islamic Studies Presented to Charles J. Adams*, edited by Wael B. Hallaq and Donald P. Little, 57–68. Leiden: Brill, 1990.

Hahn, Scott W. "Canon, Cult and Covenant: The Promise of Liturgical Hermeneutics." In *Canon and Biblical Interpretation*, edited by Craig G. Bartholomew, et al., 207–35. Grand Rapids: Zondervan, 2006.

———, ed. *Catholic Bible Dictionary*. New York: Doubleday, 2009.

———. *Covenant and Communion: The Biblical Theology of Pope Benedict XVI*. Grand Rapids: Brazos, 2009.

———. *Letter and Spirit: From Written Text to Living Word in the Liturgy*. New York: Doubleday, 2005.

———. *Scripture Matters: Essays on Reading the Bible from the Heart of the Church*. Steubenville: Emmaus Road, 2003.

———. "Worship in the Word: Toward a Liturgical Hermeneutic." *Letter & Spirit* 1 (2005) 101–36.

Hahn, Scott W., and Benjamin Wiker. *Politicizing the Bible: The Roots of Historical Criticism and the Secularization of Scripture 1300–1700*. New York: Herder & Herder, 2013.

Hammill, Graham. *The Mosaic Constitution: Political Theology and Imagination from Machiavelli to Milton*. Chicago: University of Chicago Press, 2012.

Haran, Alexandre Y. *Le lys et le globe: Messianisme dynastique et rêve impérial en France aux XVIe et XVIIe siècles*. Seyssel: Champ Vallon, 2000.

Hauerwas, Stanley. *The State of the University: Academic Knowledges and the Knowledge of God*. Oxford: Blackwell, 2007.

Hazard, Paul. *La crise de la conscience européenne, 1680-1715*. Paris: Boivin et Cie, 1935.

Heft, James. *John XXII and Papal Teaching Authority*. Lewiston: Edwin Mellen, 1986.

Hill, Harvey. "Henri Bergson and Alfred Loisy: On Mysticism and the Religious Life." In *Modernists & Mystics*, edited by C. J. T. Talar, 23–38. Washington, DC: The Catholic University of America Press, 2009.

———. "Leo XIII, Loisy, and the 'Broad School': An Early Round of the Modernist Crisis." *Catholic Historical Review* 89.1 (2003) 39–59.

———. "The Politics of Loisy's Modernist Theology." In *Catholicism Contending with Modernity: Roman Catholic Modernism and Anti-Modernism in Historical Context*, edited by Darrell Jodock, 169–90. Cambridge: Cambridge University Press, 2000.

Hoffmeier, James K. *Ancient Israel in Sinai: The Evidence for the Authenticity of the Wilderness Tradition*. Oxford: Oxford University Press, 2005.

———. *Israel in Egypt: The Evidence for the Authenticity of the Exodus Tradition*. Oxford: Oxford University Press, 1996.

Holloway, Steven W. "Biblical Assyria and Other Anxieties in the British Empire." *Journal of Religion & Society* 3 (2001) 1–21.

Homan, Michael M. "How Moses Gained and Lost the Reputation of Being the Torah's Author: Higher Criticism prior to Julius Wellhausen." In *Sacred History, Sacred Literature: Essays on Ancient Israel, the Bible, and Religion in Honor of R. E. Friedman on His Sixtieth Birthday*, edited by Shawna Dolansky, 111–32. Winona Lake: Eisenbrauns, 2008.

Idel, Moshe. "Midrashic Versus Other Forms of Jewish Hermeneutics: Some Comparative Reflections." In *The Midrashic Imagination: Jewish Exegesis, Thought, and History*, edited by Michael Fishbane, 45–58. Albany: State University of New York Press, 1993.

Israel, Jonathan I. *Enlightenment Contested: Philosophy, Modernity, and the Emancipation of Man 1670-1752*. Oxford: Oxford University Press, 2006.

———. *Radical Enlightenment: Philosophy and the Making of Modernity 1650-1750*. Oxford: Oxford University Press, 2001.

James, Susan. *Spinoza on Philosophy, Religion, and Politics: The Theologico-Political Treatise*. Oxford: Oxford University Press, 2012.

John Paul II. *Ecclesia in America* (1999). http://www.vatican.va/holy_father/john_paul_ii/apost_exhortations/documents/hf_jp-ii_exh_22011999_ecclesia-in-america_en.html.

Jones, Andrew Willard. *Before Church and State: A Study of Social Order in the Sacramental Kingdom of St. Louis IX*. Steubenville: Emmaus Academic, 2017.

Jorink, Eric. "'Horrible and Blasphemous': Isaac La Peyrère, Isaac Vossius, and the Emergence of Radical Biblical Criticism in the Dutch Republic." In *Nature and Scripture in the Abrahamic Religions: Up to 1700*, edited by Jitse M. van der Meer and Scott Mandelbrote, 429–550. Vol. 1. Leiden: Brill, 2008.

———. *Reading the Book of Nature in the Dutch Golden Age, 1575-1715*. Leiden: Brill, 2010.

BIBLIOGRAPHY

Kaplan, Yosef. "The Social Functions of the *Herem* in the Portuguese Jewish Community of Amsterdam in the Seventeenth Century." In *Dutch Jewish History*, edited by Jozeph Michman and Tirisah Levie, 111–55. Vol. 1. Jerusalem: Tel-Aviv University Press 1984.

Kasher, Rimon. "The Interpretation of Scripture in Rabbinic Literature." In *Mikra: Text, Translation, Reading & Interpretation of the Hebrew Bible in Ancient Judaism & Early Christianity*, edited by Martin J. Mulder and Harry Sysling, 547–94. Peabody, MA: Hendrickson, 2004 (1988).

Kaufmann, Yehezkel. *The Religion of Israel: From Its Beginnings to the Babylonian Exile*. Chicago: University of Chicago Press, 1960.

Kelly, J. N. D. *The Oxford Dictionary of Popes*. Oxford: Oxford University Press, 1986.

Kitchen, K. A. *On the Reliability of the Old Testament*. Grand Rapids: Eerdmans, 2003.

Klepper, Deeana Copeland. "Theories of Interpretation: The Quadriga and its Successors." In *From 1450 to 1750*, edited Euan Cameron, 418–38. Vol. 3 of *The New Cambridge History of the Bible*. Cambridge: Cambridge University Press, 2016.

Klijnsmit, Anthony J. "Amsterdam Sephardim and Hebrew Grammar in the Seventeenth Century." *Studia Rosenthaliana* 22.2 (1988) 144–64.

———. "The Problem of Normativity Solved." *Studia Spinozana* 4 (1988) 305–14.

———. "Some Seventeenth-Century Grammatical Descriptions of Hebrew." *Histoire Épistémologie Langage* 12.1 (1990) 77–101.

Kofsky, Aryeh. *Eusebius of Caesarea Against Paganism*. Leiden: Brill, 2000.

Kraus, Hans-Joachim. *Geschichte der historisch-kritischen Erforschung des Alten Testaments*. Neukirchen: Kreis Moers, 1956.

Kugel, James L. "The Bible in the University." In *The Hebrew Bible and Its Interpreters*, edited by William Henry Propp, et al., 143–65. Winona Lake, IN: Eisenbrauns, 1990.

———. *How to Read the Bible: A Guide to Scripture, Then and Now*. New York: Free Press, 2007.

Kuhn, Thomas S. *The Structure of Scientific Revolutions*. Chicago: University of Chicago Press, 2012 (1962).

La Peyrère, Isaac. *Du Rappel des Juifs*. n.p., 1643.

———. *Men before Adam. Or a Discourse upon the twelfth, thirteenth, and fourteenth Verses of the Fifth Chapter of the Epistle of the Apostle Paul to the Romans. By which are prov'd, That the first Men were created before Adam*. London: n.p., 1656.

———. *Prae-Adamitae. Sive Exercitatio super Versibus duodecimo, decimotertio, & decimoquarto, capitis quinti Epistolae D. Pauli ad Romanos. Quibus Inducuntur Primi Homines ante Adamum conditi*. n.p., 1655.

———. *Systema Theologicum, ex Prae-Adamitarum Hypothesi. Pars Prima*. n.p., 1655.

———. *A Theological Systeme Upon that Presupposition, That Men were before Adam. The First Part*. London: n.p., 1655.

Lagrée, Jacqueline, and Pierre-François Moreau. "Introduction" to *Œuvres III: Tractatus Theologico-Politicus/Traité théologico-politique*, by Baruch Spinoza, 3–17. Edited by Pierre-François Moreau. Text established by Fokke Akkerman. Translated and notes by Jacqueline Lagrée and Pierre-François Moreau. 2nd ed. Paris: Presses Universitaires de France, 2012.

Lazarus-Yafeh, Hava. *Intertwined Worlds: Medieval Islam and Bible Criticism*. Princeton: Princeton University Press, 1992.

———. "Some Neglected Aspects of Medieval Polemics against Christianity." *Harvard Theological Review* 89.1 (1996) 61–84.

Lease, Gary. "Vatican Foreign Policy and the Origins of Modernism." In *Catholicism Contending with Modernity: Roman Catholic Modernism and Anti-Modernism in Historical Context*, edited by Darrell Jodock, 31–55. Cambridge: Cambridge University Press, 2000.

Legaspi, Michael C. *The Death of Scripture and the Rise of Biblical Studies*. Oxford: Oxford University Press, 2010.

———. "'Unless You Believe, You Will Not Understand': A Brief History of Isaiah 7:9." Paper presented at the annual meeting of the Society of Biblical Literature, Boston, MA, 2008.

Leijenhorst, Cees. "Sense and Nonsense about Sense: Hobbes and the Aristotelians on Sense Perception and Imagination." In *The Cambridge Companion to Hobbes's Leviathan*, edited by Patricia Springborg, 82–108. Cambridge: Cambridge University Press, 2007.

Lessay, Franck. "Hobbes and Sacred History." In *Hobbes and History*, edited by G. A. J. Rogers and Tom Sorell, 147–59. London: Routledge, 2000.

Levenson, Jon D. *The Hebrew Bible, the Old Testament, and Historical Criticism: Jews and Christians in Biblical Studies*. Louisville: Westminster John Knox, 1993.

Levering, Matthew. *Participatory Biblical Exegesis: A Theology of Biblical Interpretation*. Notre Dame: University of Notre Dame Press, 2008.

Levy, Ze'ev. "The Problem of Normativity in Spinoza's 'Hebrew Grammar.'" *Studia Spinozana* 3 (1987) 351–90.

Livingstone, David N. *Adam's Ancestors: Race, Religion, and the Politics of Human Origins*. Baltimore: Johns Hopkins University Press, 2008.

———. "Cultural Politics and the Racial Cartographics of Human Origins." *Transactions of the Institute of British Geographers* 35 (2010) 204–21.

Ljamai, Abdelilah. *Ibn Hazm et la polémique islamo-chrétienne dans l'histoire de l'islam*. Leiden: Brill, 2003.

Loisy, Alfred. *L'Évangile et l'Église*. Paris: A. Picard and Sons, 1902.

Lorberbaum, Menachem. "Spinoza's Theological-Political Problem." In *Political Hebraism: Judaic Sources in Early Modern Political Thought*, edited by Gordon Schochet, et al., 167–88. Jerusalem: Shalem, 2008.

Löwenbrück, Anna-Ruth. "Johann David Michaelis et les débuts de la critique biblique." In *Le siècle des Lumières et la Bible*, edited by Yvon Belaval and Dominique Bourel, 113–28. Paris: Beauchesne, 1986.

Luther, Martin. "Von weltlicher Obrigkeit, wie weit man ihr Gehorsam schuldig sei." In *D. Martin Luthers Werke: Kritische Gesamtausgabe Band 11*, 246–80. Weimer: Hermann Böhlaus Nachfolger, 1900.

Machinist, Peter. "The Road Not Taken: Wellhausen and Assyriology." In *Homeland and Exile: Biblical and Near Eastern Studies in Honour of Bustenay Oded*, edited by Gershon Galil, et al., 469–532. Leiden: Brill, 2009.

Maddox, Graham. "The Secular Reformation and the Influence of Machiavelli." *Journal of Religion* 82.4 (2002) 539–62.

Malcolm, Noel. *Aspects of Hobbes*. Oxford: Oxford University Press, 2002.

———. "Hobbes, Sandys, and the Virginia Company." *Historical Journal* 24 (1981) 297–321.

———. "*Leviathan*, the Pentateuch, and the Origins of Modern Biblical Criticism." In *Leviathan After 350 Years*, edited by Tom Sorell and Luc Foisneau, 241–64. Oxford: Oxford University Press, 2004.

———. *Reason of State, Propaganda, and the Thirty Years' War: An Unknown Translation by Thomas Hobbes.* Oxford: Oxford University Press, 2007.

———. "A Summary Biography of Hobbes." In *The Cambridge Companion to Hobbes,* edited by Tom Sorell, 13–44. Cambridge: Cambridge University Press, 1996.

———, ed. *Thomas Hobbes: Leviathan.* 3 vols. Oxford: Oxford University Press, 2012.

Malet, André. *Le traité théologico-politique de Spinoza et la pensée biblique.* Paris: Sociéte les belles letters, 1966.

Malherbe, Michel. "Hobbes et la Bible." In *Le Grand Siècle et la Bible,* edited by Jean-Robert Armogathe, 691–99. Paris: Beauchesne, 1989.

Manrique Charry, Juan Francisco. "La herencia de Bacon en la doctrina spinocista del lenguaje." *Universitas Philosophica* 54 (2010) 121–30.

Manuel, Frank. *The Broken Staff: Judaism through Christian Eyes.* Cambridge: Harvard University Press, 1992.

Marchand, Suzanne. *Down from Olympus: Archaeology and Philhellenism in Germany, 1750–1970.* Princeton: Princeton University Press, 1996.

Marius, Richard. *Martin Luther: The Christian between God and Death.* Cambridge: Belknap, 1999.

Martinich, A. P. "The Bible and Protestantism in *Leviathan*." In *The Cambridge Companion to Hobbes's Leviathan,* edited by Patricia Springborg, 375–91. Cambridge: Cambridge University Press, 2007.

———. *Hobbes: A Biography.* Cambridge: Cambridge University Press, 1999.

Marx, Anthony W. *Faith in Nation: Exclusionary Origins of Nationalism.* Oxford: Oxford University Press, 2003.

Marx, Steven. "Moses and Machiavellism." *Journal of the American Academy of Religion* 65.3 (1997) 551–71.

Masuzawa, Tomoko. *The Invention of World Religions: Or, How European Universalism Was Preserved in the Language of Pluralism.* Chicago: University of Chicago Press, 2005.

Mayer, Cornelius P. "Prinzipien der Hermeneutik Augustins und daraus sich ergebende Probleme." *Forum Katholische Theologie* 1 (1985) 197–211.

Mazza, Enrico. *Mystagogy: A Theology of Liturgy in the Patristic Age.* Translated by Matthew J. O'Connell. New York: Pueblo, 1989.

McDermott, Ryan. "Henri de Lubac's Genealogy of Modern Exegesis and Nicholas of Lyra's Literal Sense of Scripture." *Modern Theology* 29.1 (2013) 124–56.

McKane, William. *Selected Christian Hebraists.* Cambridge: Cambridge University Press, 1989.

Miethke, Jürgen. "Der Kampf Ludwigs des Bayern mit Papst und avignonesischer Kurie in seiner Bedeutung für die deutsche Geschichte." In *Kaiser Ludwig der Bayer. Konflikte, Weichenstellungen und Wahrnehmung seiner Herrschaft,* edited by Hermann Nehlsen and Hans-Georg Hermann, 39–74. Paderborn: Schöningh, 2002.

Milbank, John. *Theology and Social Theory: Beyond Secular Reason.* Oxford: Blackwell, 1990.

Minnis, A.J. "Material Swords and Literal Lights: The Status of Allegory in William of Ockham's *Breviloquium* on Papal Power." In *With Reverence for the Word: Medieval Scriptural Exegesis in Judaism, Christianity, and Islam,* edited by Jane Dammen McAuliffe, et al., 292–308. Oxford: Oxford University Press, 2003.

———. "*Quadruplex Sensus, Multiplex Modus*: Scriptural Sense and Mode in Medieval Scholastic Exegesis." In *Interpretation and Allegory: Antiquity to the Modern Period*, edited by Jon Whitman, 231–56. Leiden: Brill, 2000.

Mirri, F. Saverio. *Richard Simon e il metodo storico-critico di B. Spinoza. Storia di un libro e di una polemica sulla sfondo delle lotte politico-religiose della Francia di Luigi XIV*. Florence: Felice Le Monnier, 1972.

Misner, Paul. "Social Modernism in Italy." In *Political and Social Modernism*, edited by Ronald Burke, et al., 18–35. Mobile: Spring Hill College, 1988.

Momigliano, Arnaldo. "Religious History Without Frontiers: J. Wellhausen, U. Wilamowitz, and E. Schwartz." *History and Theory* 21.4 (1982) 49–64.

Moorman, Mary C. *Indulgences: Luther, Catholicism, and the Imputation of Merit*. Steubenville: Emmaus Academic, 2017.

Moreau, Pierre-François. "Le méthode d'interprétation de l'Écriture Sainte: déterminations et limites." In *Spinoza: science et religion*, edited by Renée Bouveresse, 109–14. Paris: Vrin, 1988.

Morrow, Jeffrey L. "The Acid of History: La Peyrère, Hobbes, Spinoza, and the Separation of Faith and Reason in Modern Biblical Studies." *Heythrop Journal* 58.2 (2017) 169–80.

———. *Alfred Loisy and Modern Biblical Studies*. Washington, DC: Catholic University of America Press, 2019.

———. "Averroism, Nominalism, and Mechanization: Hahn and Wiker's Unmasking of Historical Criticism's Political Agenda by Laying Bare its Philosophical Roots." *Nova et Vetera* 14.4 (2016) 1293–340.

———. "*Dei verbum* in Light of the History of Catholic Biblical Interpretation." *Josephinum Journal of Theology* 23.1/2 (2016) 227–49.

———. "Evangelical Catholics and Catholic Biblical Scholarship: An Examination of Scott Hahn's Canonical, Liturgical, and Covenantal Biblical Exegesis." PhD dissertation, University of Dayton, 2007.

———. *Jesus' Resurrection: A Jewish Convert Examines the Evidence*. Toledo, OH: Principium Institute, 2017.

———. "The Modernist Crisis and the Shifting of Catholic Views on Biblical Inspiration." *Letter & Spirit* 6 (2010) 265–80.

———. "Religion and Empire: Loisy's Use of 'Religion' Prior to his Excommunication." In *Constructing Nineteenth-Century Religion: Literary, Historical, and Religious Studies in Dialogue*, edited by Joshua King and Winter Jade Werner. Columbus: Ohio State University Press, forthcoming.

———. "Secularization, Objectivity, and Enlightenment Scholarship: The Theological and Political Origins of Modern Biblical Studies." *Logos* 18.1 (2015) 14–32.

———. "Spinoza and the Theo-Political Implications of his Freedom to Philosophize." *New Blackfriars* 99.1081 (2018) 374–87.

———. *Theology, Politics, and Exegesis: Essays on the History of Modern Biblical Criticism*. Eugene, OR: Pickwick, 2017.

———. "Thomas More on the Sadness of Christ: From Mystagogy to Martyrdom." *Heythrop Journal* 58 (2017) 365–73.

———. *Three Skeptics and the Bible: La Peyrère, Hobbes, Spinoza, and the Reception of Modern Biblical Criticism*. Eugene, OR: Pickwick, 2016.

———. "The Untold History of Modern Biblical Scholarship's Pre-Enlightenment Secular Origins." *Journal of Theological Interpretation* 8.1 (2014) 145–55.

Muller, Richard A. "The Hermeneutic of Promise and Fulfillment in Calvin's Exegesis of the Old Testament Prophecies of the Kingdom." In *The Bible in the Sixteenth Century*, edited by David C. Steinmetz, 68-82. Durham: Duke University Press, 1996.

Müller, Sascha. *Kritik und Theologie: Christliche Glaubens und Schrifthermeneutik nach Richard Simon*. St Ottilien: EOS, 2004.

———. *Richard Simon (1638-1712): Exeget, Theologe, Philosoph und Historiker*. Bamberg: Echter, 2006.

Nadler, Steven. "The Bible Hermeneutics of Baruch de Spinoza." In *From the Renaissance to the Enlightenment*, edited by Magne Sæbø, 827-36. Vol. 2 of *Hebrew Bible/Old Testament: The History of Its Interpretation*. Göttingen: Vandenhoeck & Ruprecht, 2008.

———. *A Book Forged in Hell: Spinoza's Scandalous Treatise and the Birth of the Secular Age*. Princeton: Princeton University Press, 2011.

———. *Spinoza: A Life*. Cambridge: Cambridge University Press, 1999.

Nahkola, Aulikki. "The *Memoires* of Moses and the Genesis of Method in Biblical Criticism: Astruc's Contribution." In *Sacred Conjectures: The Context and Legacy of Robert Lowth and Jean Astruc*, edited by John Jarick, 204-20. London: T&T Clark, 2007.

Nehlsen, Hermann. "Die Rolle Ludwigs des Bayern und seiner Berater Marsilius von Padua und Wilhelm von Ockham im Tiroler Ehekonflikt." In *Kaiser Ludwig der Bayer. Konflikte, Weichenstellungen und Wahrnehmung seiner Herrschaft*, edited by Hermann Nehlsen and Hans-Georg Hermann, 285-328. Paderborn: Schöningh, 2002.

Nellen, H. J. M. "Growing Tension between Church Doctrines and Critical Exegesis of the Old Testament." In *From the Renaissance to the Enlightenment*, edited by Magne Sæbø, 802-26. Vol. 2 of *Hebrew Bible/Old Testament: The History of Its Interpretation*. Göttingen: Vandenhoeck & Ruprecht, 2008.

Nelson, Eric. *The Hebrew Republic: Jewish Sources and the Transformation of European Political Thought*. Cambridge: Harvard University Press, 2010.

Novick, Peter. *That Noble Dream: The "Objectivity Question" and the American Historical Profession*. Cambridge: Cambridge University Press, 1988.

Noyes, John K. "Goethe on Cosmopolitanism and Colonialism: *Bildung* and the Dialectic of Critical Mobility." *Eighteenth-Century Studies* 39 (2006) 443-62.

O'Connell, Marvin R. "The Bishopric of Monaco, 1902: A Revision." *Catholic Historical Review* 71 (1985) 26-51.

———. *Critics on Trial: An Introduction to the Catholic Modernist Crisis*. Washington, DC: Catholic University of America Press, 1994.

O'Loughlin, Thomas. "The Controversy over Methuselah's Death: Proto-Chronology and the Origins of the Western Concept of Inerrancy." *Recherches de théologie ancienne et médiévale* 62 (1995) 182-225.

Osier, Jean Pierre. "L'herméneutique de Hobbes et de Spinoza." *Studia Spinozana* 3 (1987) 319-47.

Pacchi, Arrigo. "Hobbes e l'epicureismo." *Rivista critica di storia della filosofia* 33 (1975) 54-71.

———. "Hobbes e la filologia biblica al servizio dello Stato." *Annali di storia dell'esegesi* 7.1 (1990) 277-92.

———. "*Leviathan* and Spinoza's *Tractatus* on Revelation: Some Elements for a Comparison." *History of European Ideas* 10.5 (1989) 577-93.

Paganini, Gianni. "Hobbes's Critique of the Doctrines of Essences and Its Sources." In *The Cambridge Companion to Hobbes's Leviathan*, edited by Patricia Springborg, 337–57. Cambridge: Cambridge University Press, 2007.

Parente, Fausto. "Isaac de La Peyrère interprète de Paul: Pourquoi le *Rappel des Juifs* a-t-il été presque entièrement détruit au moment de sa publication?" *Revue des études juives* 167 (2008) 169–86.

———. "Isaac de La Peyrère e Richard Simon: Osservazioni preliminary ad uno studio del Ms. Chantilly, Musée de Condé, n. 191 (698): *De Iuifs Elus, Reietés, et Rapelés* di Isaac de La Peyrère." In *La geografia dei saperi: Scritti in memoria di Dino Pastine*, edited by Domenico Ferraro and Gianna Gigliotti, 161–82. Florence: La Lettere, 2000.

Parkin, Jon. "The Reception of Hobbes's *Leviathan*." In *The Cambridge Companion to Hobbes's Leviathan*, edited by Patricia Springborg, 441–59. Cambridge: Cambridge University Press, 2007.

Pasto, James. "Islam's 'Strange Secret Sharer': Orientalism, Judaism, and the Jewish Question." *Comparative Studies in Society and History* 40 (1998) 437–74.

———. "W. M. L. de Wette and the Invention of Post-Exilic Judaism: Political Historiography and Christian Allegory in Nineteenth-Century German Biblical Scholarship." In *Jews, Antiquity, and the Nineteenth-Century Imagination*, edited by Hayim Lapin and Dale B. Martin, 33–52. Bethesda: University Press of Maryland, 2003.

———. "When the End is the Beginning? Or When the Biblical Past is the Political Present: Some Thoughts on Ancient Israel, 'Post-Exilic Judaism,' and the Politics of Biblical Scholarship." *Scandinavian Journal of the Old Testament* 12 (1998) 157–202.

Pickstock, Catherine. *After Writing: On the Liturgical Consummation of Philosophy*. Oxford: Blackwell, 1998.

Pietsch, Andreas Nikolaus. *Isaac La Peyrère: Bibelkritik, Philosemitismus und Patronage in der Gelehrtenrepublik des 17. Jahrhunderts*. Berlin: Walter de Gruyter, 2012.

Pitre, Brant. "The Mystery of God's Word: Inspiration, Inerrancy, and the Interpretation of Scripture." *Letter & Spirit* 6 (2010) 47–66.

Pius X. *Pascendi Dominici Gregis*. In *1903–1939*, edited by Claudia Carlen, 71–98. Vol. 3 of *The Papal Encyclicals*. Raleigh, North Carolina: McGrath, 1981.

Popkin, Richard H. "The First Published Reaction to Spinoza's *Tractatus*: Col. J. B. Stouppe, the Condé Circle, and the Rev. Jean Lebrun." In *The Spinozistic Heresy: The Debate on the Tractatus Theologico-Politicus, 1670–1677*, edited by Paolo Christofolini, 6–12. Amsterdam and Maarssen: APA-Holland University Press, 1995.

———. *The History of Scepticism: From Savonarola to Bayle*. Oxford: Oxford University Press, 2003.

———. *Isaac La Peyrère (1596–1676): His Life, Work and Influence*. Leiden: Brill, 1987.

———. "Jewish-Christian Relations in the Sixteenth and Seventeenth Centuries: The Conception of the Messiah." *Jewish History* 6 (1992) 163–77.

———. "Millenarianism and Nationalism—A Case Study: Isaac La Peyrère." In *Continental Millenarians: Protestants, Catholics, Heretics*, edited by John Christian Laursen and Richard H. Popkin, 74–84. Vol. 4 of *Millenarianism and Messianism in Early Modern European Culture*. Dordrecht: Kluwer Academic, 2001.

———. "The Pre-Adamite Theory in the Renaissance." In *Philosophy and Humanism: Renaissance Essays in Honor of Paul Oskar Kristeller*, edited by Edward P. Mahoney, 50–69. Leiden: Brill, 1976.

———. *Spinoza*. Oxford: Oneworld, 2004.
———. "Spinoza and La Peyrère." *Southwestern Journal of Philosophy* 8 (1977) 188–91.
———. *The Third Force in Seventeenth-Century Thought*. Leiden: Brill, 1992.
Portier, William L. "Church Unity and National Traditions: The Challenge to the Modern Papacy, 1682–1870." In *The Papacy and the Church in the United States*, edited by Bernard Cooke, 25–54. New York: Paulist, 1989.
———. *Divided Friends: Portraits of the Roman Catholic Modernist Crisis in the United States*. Washington, DC: Catholic University of America Press, 2013.
Poulat, Émile. *Intégrisme et Catholicisme Intégral: Un réseau secret international antimoderniste: La «Sapinière» (1909–1921)*. Paris: Casterman, 1969.
Preus, J. Samuel. "A Hidden Opponent in Spinoza's *Tractatus*." *Harvard Theological Review* 88 (1995) 361–88.
———. *Spinoza and the Irrelevance of Biblical Authority*. Cambridge: Cambridge University Press, 2001.
Pulcini, Theodore. *Exegesis as Polemical Discourse: Ibn Ḥazm on Jewish and Christian Scriptures*. Atlanta: Scholars, 1998.
Quennehen, Élisabeth. "Lapeyrère, la Chine et la chronologie biblique." *La Lettre clandestine* 9 (2000) 243–55.
———. "'L'auteur des *Préadamites*,' Isaac Lapeyrère. Essai biographique." In *Dissidents, excentriques et marginaux de l'Âge classique: Autour de Cyrano de Bergerac: Bouquet offert à Madeleine Alcover*, edited by Patricia Harry, et al., 349–73. Paris: Honoré Champion Éditeur, 2006.
Ramón Guerrero, Rafael. "Filósofos hispano-musulmanes y Spinoza: Avempace y Abentofail." In *Spinoza y España: Actas del Congreso Internacional sobre "Relaciones entre Spinoza y España" (Almagro, 5–7 noviembre 1992)*, edited by Atilano Domínguez, 125–32. Almagro: Ediciones de la Universidad de Castilla-La Mancha, 1994.
Ratzinger, Joseph (Benedict XVI). *Behold the Pierced One*. San Francisco: Ignatius, 1986 (1984).
———. "Biblical Interpretation in Conflict." In *God's Word: Scripture—Tradition—Office*, 91–126. San Francisco: Ignatius, 2008 (2005).
———. "Biblical Interpretation in Crisis. On the Question of the Foundations and Approaches of Exegesis Today." In *Biblical Interpretation in Crisis: The Ratzinger Conference on Bible and Church*, edited by Richard John Neuhaus, 1–23. Grand Rapids: Eerdmans, 1989.
———. *Jesus of Nazareth: From the Baptism in the Jordan to the Transfiguration*. New York: Doubleday, 2007.
———. *Jesus of Nazareth II: Holy Week: From the Entrance Into Jerusalem to the Resurrection*. San Francisco: Ignatius, 2011.
———. *Jesus of Nazareth III: The Infancy Narratives*. San Francisco: Ignatius, 2012.
———. *The Nature and Mission of Theology: Essays to Orient Theology in Today's Debates*. Translated by Adrian Walker. San Francisco: Ignatius, 1995 (1993).
———. *Schriftauslegung im Widerstreit*. Freiburg im Breisgau: Herder, 1989.
———. "Verbum Domini." *Acta Apostolicae Sedis* 102.11 (2010) 681–787.
Rendsburg, Gary A. *The Redaction of Genesis*. Winona Lake, IN: Eisenbrauns, 1986.
Reventlow, Henning Graf. *The Authority of the Bible and the Rise of the Modern World*. London: SCM, 1984.

BIBLIOGRAPHY

———. *Bibelautorität und Geist der Moderne, Die bedeutung des Bibelverständnisses für die geistesgeschichtliche und politische Entwicklung in England von der Reformation bis zur Aufklärung.* Göttingen: Vandenhoek & Ruprecht, 1980.

———. *Epochen der Bibelauslegung Band IV: Von der Aufklärung bis zum 20. Jahrhundert.* Munich: C.H. Beck, 2001.

———. *From the Enlightenment to the Twentieth Century.* Vol. 4 of *History of Biblical Interpretation.* Atlanta: Society of Biblical Literature, 2010.

———. "Richard Simon und seine Bedeutung fur die kritische Erforschung der Bibel." In *Historische Kritik in der Theologie: Beitrage zu ihrer Geschichte*, edited by Georg Schwaiger, 11–36. Göttingen: Vandenhoeck & Ruprecht, 1980.

Rif'at, Nurshif. "Ibn Ḥazm on Jews and Judaism." Dissertation, Exeter University, 1988.

Rocha, Biff, and Jeffrey L. Morrow. "Dancing on the Wall: An Analysis of Barack Obama's 'Call to Renewal' Keynote Address." In *What Democrats Talk About When They Talk About God: Religious Communication in Democratic Party Politics*, edited by David Weiss, 129–54. Lanham, MD: Lexington Books, 2010.

Rodrigues, M. A. "Algumas notas sobre o *Compendium Grammatices Hebraeae* de Baruch Spinoza." *Helmantica* 49 (1998) 111–29.

Rogers, G. A. J. "Hobbes, History and Wisdom." In *Hobbes and History*, edited by G. A. J. Rogers and Tom Sorell, 73–81. London: Routledge, 2000.

Rogerson, John W. *Old Testament Criticism in the Nineteenth Century: England and Germany.* London: Fortress, 1985 (1984).

Rosenthal, Frank. "Heinrich von Oyta and Biblical Criticism in the Fourteenth Century." *Speculum* 25.2 (1950) 178–83.

Rosenthal, Michael A. "Miracles, Wonder, and the State." In *Spinoza's Theological-Political Treatise: A Critical Guide*, edited by Yitzhak Y. Melamed and Michael A. Rosenthal, 231–49. Cambridge: Cambridge University Press, 2010.

Sacksteder, William. "How Much of Hobbes Might Spinoza Have Read?" *Southwestern Journal of Philosophy* 11 (1980) 25–39.

Sæbø, Magne, ed. *From the Renaissance to the Enlightenment.* Vol. 2 of *Hebrew Bible/Old Testament: The History of Its Interpretation.* Göttingen: Vandenhoeck & Ruprecht, 2008.

Schindler, David L. *Heart of the World, Center of the Church: Communio Ecclesiology, Liberalism, and Liberation.* Grand Rapids: Eerdmans, 1996.

Schuhmann, Karl. "Hobbes's Concept of History." In *Hobbes and History*, edited by G. A. J. Rogers and Tom Sorell, 3–24. London: Routledge, 2000.

———. "Methodenfragen bei Spinoza und Hobbes: Zum Problem des Einflusses." *Studia Spinozana* 3 (1987) 47–86.

Schwetizer, Albert. *Vom Reimaruz zu Wrede. Eine Geschichte der Leben Jesu forschung.* Tübingen: J. C. B. Mohr, 1906.

Scribner, R.W., and C. Scott Dixon. *The German Reformation.* 2nd ed. New York: Palgrave Macmillan, 2003.

Shadle, Matthew A. "Cavanaugh on the Church and the Modern State: An Appraisal." *Horizons* 37.2 (2010) 246–70.

Sheehan, Jonathan. *The Enlightenment Bible: Translation, Scholarship, Culture.* Princeton: Princeton University Press, 2005.

Silberman, Neil Asher. *Digging for God and Country: Exploration, Archeology, and the Secret Struggle for the Holy Land, 1799–1917.* New York: Knopf, 1982.

Simon, Christian. "History As a Case-Study of the Relations Between University Professors and the State in Germany." In *Biblical Studies and the Shifting of Paradigms: 1850–1914*, edited by Henning Graf Reventlow and William Farmer, 168–96. Sheffield: Sheffield Academic, 1995.

Simonetti, Manlio. "Lermeneutica biblica di Agostino." *Annali di storia dell'esegesi* 12 (1995) 393–418.

Sinai, Nicolai. "Spinoza and Beyond: Some Reflections on Historical-Critical Method." In *Kritische Religionsphilosophie: Eine Gedenkschrift für Friedrich Niewöhner*, edited by Wilhelm Schmidt-Biggemann and Georges Tamer, 193–213. Berlin: de Gruyter, 2010.

Skinner, Quentin. *Reason and Rhetoric in the Philosophy of Hobbes*. Cambridge: Cambridge University Press, 1997.

Sommerville, Johann P. "Hobbes, Selden, Erastianism, and the History of the Jews." In *Hobbes and History*, edited by G. A. J. Rogers and Tom Sorell, 160–88. London: Routledge, 2000.

Sorell, Tom. "Hobbes's Uses of the History of Philosophy." In *Hobbes and History*, edited by G. A. J. Rogers and Tom Sorell, 82–96. London: Routledge, 2000.

Spinoza, Baruch. *Compendium Grammatices Linguae Hebraeae*. Vol 1. of *Benedict de Spinoza Opera*. Edited by Carl Gebhardt. Heidelberg: Carl Winter, 1925.

———. *Œuvres III: Tractatus Theologico-Politicus/Traité théologico-politique*. 2nd ed. Edited by Pierre-François Moreau. Text established by Fokke Akkerman. Translated and notes by Jacqueline Lagrée and Pierre-François Moreau. Paris: Presses Universitaires de France, 2012.

———. *Theological-Political Treatise*. Edited by Jonathan Israel. Translated by Michael Silverthorne and Jonathan Israel. Cambridge: Cambridge University Press, 2007.

Springborg, Patricia. "A Critical Response to the Hobbes Symposium, *Political Theory*, Vol. 36, 2008." *Political Theory* 37.5 (2009) 676–88.

———. "Hobbes and Epicurean Religion." In *Der Garten und die Moderne: Epikureische Moral und Politik vom Humanismus bis zur Aufklärung*, edited by Gianni Paganini and Edoardo Tortarolo, 161–214. Stuttgart: Rommann-holzboog Verlag, 2004.

———. "Hobbes and Historiography: Why the Future, He Says, Does Not Exist." In *Hobbes and History*, edited by G. A. J. Rogers and Tom Sorell, 44–72. London: Routledge, 2000.

———. "Hobbes's Theory of Civil Religion." In *Pluralismo e religione civile*, edited by Gianni Paganini and Edoardo Tortarolo, 61–98. Milan: Bruno Mondatori, 2003.

Stallsworth, Paul T. "The Story of an Encounter." In *Biblical Interpretation in Crisis: The Ratzinger Conference on Bible and Church*, edited by Richard John Neuhaus, 102–90. Grand Rapids: Eerdmans, 1989.

Starobinski-Safran, Esther. "Raison et conflits de traditions." In *L'Europe et les Juifs*, edited by Esther Benbassa and Pierre Gisel, 95–128. Geneva: Éditions Labor et Fides, 2002.

Steinmetz, David C. "John Calvin as an Interpreter of the Bible." In *Calvin and the Bible*, edited by Donald K. McKim, 282–91. Cambridge: Cambridge University Press, 2006.

———. *Luther in Context*. Bloomington: Indiana University Press, 1986.

Strayer, Joseph R. *On the Medieval Origins of the Modern State*. Princeton: Princeton University Press, 1970.

Stroumsa, Guy G. "Richard Simon: From Philology to Comparatism." *Archiv für Religionsgeschichte* 3 (2001) 89–107.

Subrahmanyam, Sanjay. "Intertwined Histories: *Crónica* and *Tārīkh* in the Sixteenth-Century Indian Ocean World." *History & Theory* 49.4 (2010) 118–45.

Synan, Edward. "The Four 'Senses' and Four Exegetes." In *With Reverence for the Word: Medieval Scriptural Exegesis in Judaism, Christianity, and Islam*, edited by Jane Dammen McAuliffe, et al., 225–36. Oxford: Oxford University Press, 2003.

Tabet Balady, Miguel Angel. "La hermenéutica bíblica de san Agustín en la carta 82 a san Jerónimo." In *San Agustín: Meditación de un Centenario*, edited by José Oroz Reta, 181–93. Salamanca: Universidad Pontificia de Salamanca, 1987.

Talmage, Frank. "Apples of Gold: The Inner Meaning of Sacred Texts in Medieval Judaism." In *Jewish Spirituality: From the Bible Through the Middle Ages*, edited by Arthur Green, 313–55. New York: Crossroad, 1994.

Tanner, Norman P., SJ, ed. *Decrees of the Ecumenical Councils*. 2 vols. Washington, DC: Georgetown University Press, 1990.

Taylor, Charles. *A Secular Age*. Cambridge: Harvard University Press, 2007.

Tierney, Brian. *Origins of Papal Infallibility, 1150–1350: A Study on the Concepts of Infallibility, Sovereignty and Tradition in the Middle Ages*. Leiden: Brill, 1972.

Tilley, Maureen A. "Understanding Augustine Misunderstanding Tyconius." *Studia Patristica* 27 (1993) 405–408.

———. "The Use of Scripture in Christian North Africa: An Examination of Donatist Hermeneutics." PhD dissertation, Duke University, 1989.

Titzmann, Michael. "Herausforderungen der biblischen Hermeneutik in der Frühen Neuzeit: Die neuen Diskurse der Wissenschaft und der Philosophie." In *Geschichte der Hermeneutik und die Methodik der textinterpretierenden Disziplinen*, edited by Jörg Schönert and Friedrich Vollhardt, 119–56. Berlin: Walter de Gruyter, 2005.

Torrell, Jean-Pierre, OP. *Initiation à saint Thomas d'Aquin: Sa personne et son oeuvre*. 2nd ed. Fribourg: Editions Universitaires Fribourg, 2002 (1993).

Tricaud, François. "L'ancien testament et le *Léviathan* de Hobbes: une cohabitation difficile." *Rivista di storia della filosofia* 2 (1999) 229–38.

Troeltsch, Ernst. "On Historical and Dogmatic Method in Theology." In *Religion in History*, by Ernst Troeltsch, 11–32. Translated by J. Adams and W. Bense. Minneapolis: Fortress, 1991.

Troilo, Erminio. "L'averroismo di Marsilio da Padova." In *Marsilio da Padova. Studi raccolti nel VI centenario della morte*, edited by Aldo Checchini and Norberto Bobbio, 47–77. Rome: Cedam, 1942.

Tuchman, Barbara. *The March of Folly: From Troy to Vietnam*. New York: Alfred A. Knopf, 1984.

Tuck, Richard. "Hobbes and Tacitus." In *Hobbes and History*, edited by G. A. J. Rogers and Tom Sorell, 99–111. London: Routledge, 2000.

van Asselt, Willem. "Adam en Eva als laatkomers De pre-adamitische speculaties van Isaac La Peyrère (1596–1676)." In *Adam en Eva in het paradijs. Actuele visies op man en vrouw uit 2000 jaar christelijke theologie*, edited by Harm Goris and Susanne Hennecke, 99–115. Zoetermeer: Meinema, 2005.

van Bunge, Wiep. *From Stevin to Spinoza: An Essay on Philosophy in the Seventeenth-Century Dutch Republic*. Leiden: Brill, 2001.

van der Coelen, Peter. "Pictures for the People? Bible Illustrations and their Audience." In *Lay Bible in Europe 1450–1800*, edited by Mathijs Lamberigts and A. A. den Hollander, 185–205. Leuven: Leuven University Press and Peeters, 2006.

Vick, Brian. "Greek Origins and Organic Metaphors: Ideals of Cultural Autonomy in Neo-Humanist Germany from Winckelmann to Curtius." *Journal of the History of Ideas* 63.3 (2002) 483–500.

Vlessing, Odette. "The Excommunication of Baruch Spinoza: A Conflict Between Jewish and Dutch Law." *Studia Spinozana* 13 (1997) 15–47.

———. "The Jewish Community in Transition: From Acceptance to Emancipation." *Studia Rosenthaliana* 30 (1996) 195–211.

———. "New Light on the Earliest History of the Amsterdam Portuguese Jews." In *Dutch Jewish History*, ed. Jozeph Michman, 43–75. Vol. 3. Assen: Van Gorcum, 1993.

Waldstein, Michael Maria. "*Analogia Verbi*: The Truth of Scripture in Rudolf Bultmann and Raymond Brown." *Letter & Spirit* 6 (2010) 93–140.

Walfish, Barry D. "An Introduction to Medieval Jewish Biblical Interpretation." In *With Reverence for the Word: Medieval Scriptural Exegesis in Judaism, Christianity, and Islam*, edited by Jane Dammen McAuliffe, et al., 3–12. Oxford: Oxford University Press, 2003.

Walther, Manfred. "Biblische Hermeneutik und historische Erklärung: Lodewijk Meyer und Benedikt de Spinoza über Norm, Methode und Ergebnis wissenschaftliche Bibelauslegung." *Studia Spinozana* 11 (1995) 227–300.

Waugh, Evelyn. *Brideshead Revisited*. New York: Back Bay, 1999 (1944).

Wellhausen, J. *Prolegomena zur Geschichte Israels*. 5th ed. Berlin: Georg Reimer, 1899 (1882).

Whybray, R. N. *The Making of the Pentateuch: A Methodological Study*. Sheffield: Sheffield Academic, 1987.

Wiker, Benjamin. *Moral Darwinism: How We Became Hedonists*. Downers Grove: InterVarsity, 2002.

Wilken, Robert Louis. *The Spirit of Early Christian Thought: Seeking the Face of God*. New Haven: Yale University Press, 2003.

Williams, Megan Hale. "Lessons from Jerome's Jewish Teachers: Exegesis and Cultural Interaction in Late Antique Palestine." In *Jewish Biblical Interpretation and Cultural Exchange: Comparative Exegesis in Context*, edited by Natalie B. Dohrmann and David Stern, 66–86. Philadelphia: University of Pennsylvania Press, 2008.

Williamson, George S. *The Longing for Myth in Germany: Religion and Aesthetic Culture from Romanticism to Nietzsche*. Chicago: University of Chicago Press, 2004.

Wolfson, Harry Austryn. *The Philosophy of Spinoza: Unfolding the Latent Processes of His Reasoning*. Vol 1. Cambridge: Harvard University Press, 1934.

Woodbridge, John D. "Richard Simon le «père de la critique biblique.»" In *Le Grand Siècle et la Bible*, edited by Jean Robert Armogathe, 193–206. Paris: Beauchesne, 1989.

Yamauchi, Edwin M. "An Ancient Historian's View of Christianity." In *Professors Who Believe: The Spiritual Journeys of Christian Faculty*, edited by Paul M. Anderson, 192–99. Downers Grove: InterVarsity, 1998.

———. "The Episode of the Magi." In *Chronos, Kairos, Christos: Nativity and Chronological Studies Presented to Jack Finegan*, edited by Jerry Vardaman and Edwin M. Yamauchi, 15–39. Winona Lake, Indiana: Eisenbrauns, 1989.

———. *Gnostic Ethics and Mandaean Origins*. Cambridge: Harvard University Press, 1970.

Yovel, Yirmiyahu. *Spinoza and Other Heretics I: The Marrano of Reason*. Princeton: Princeton University Press, 1989.

BIBLIOGRAPHY

———. *Spinoza and Other Heretics II: The Adventures of Immanence*. Princeton: Princeton University Press, 1989.
Zac, Sylvain. *Spinoza et l'interprétation de l'Écriture*. Paris: Presses universitaires de France, 1965.

Subject Index

Abelard, Peter, 102
Astruc, Jean, 82, 83n25
Averroism, 11, 16–17, 19, 24, 26, 56, 58, 63–64, 66, 70, 72–73, 78–79

Christina of Sweden, Queen, 37, 41
Condé, Prince of, 37–38, 41, 52

Dei Verbum, 76n3, 87
Descartes, René, 9, 19, 37, 55–60, 63–65, 70–71
Documentary Hypothesis, 2–4, 6, 36

Eichhorn, Johann Gottfried, 54, 104
English Civil Wars, 60, 68
Enlightenment, 13, 19, 32, 35–36, 53–54, 56, 62, 94, 100, 103, 105n55, 106
Ezra, 4

Henry VIII, 9, 12, 32–34, 56
Hobbes, Thomas, 6–9, 11n4, 13, 18, 30, 34–37, 40, 42–50, 52–56, 59–62, 65, 69–70, 81–82, 102n44, 107
Hus, Jan, 22

inspiration, 9, 43n35, 74, 76–78, 86–91, 107–108

John XXII, Pope, 15, 18, 79

Locke, John, 9, 13, 47, 55–56, 68–73

Machiavelli, Niccolò, 11–12, 22–25, 32, 34–35, 45n46, 56–57, 61–63, 66, 72–74, 80

Marsilius of Padua, 8, 11–14, 16–20, 22, 26, 29, 32, 34, 57–58, 60–61, 79, 84, 102
Michaelis, Johann David, 82, 83n25, 104
Modernist Crisis, 9, 74–77, 84–91, 108

nominalism, 11, 20, 22, 26, 47, 58n16, 61, 79

Ockham, William of, 8, 10–12, 14, 16, 18–20, 22, 25, 29, 58–59n16, 79–80, 84, 102

Pentateuch, 2, 4–5, 23–24, 36, 40, 44, 48, 50, 63, 78, 82–83

Reformation, 9–10, 12, 17, 20–22, 25–27, 31–32, 34, 80–81, 84, 93, 95, 101, 107
Reimarus, Hermann Samuel, 25

Scaliger, Joseph, 38, 49n59
secularization, x, 9, 13, 20, 26, 92, 94–95, 98, 108
Simon, Richard, ix, 6–7, 9, 11n4, 55–56, 67–70, 81–82

Toland, John, 9, 55–56, 72–74, 107
Tyrrell, George, 84

wars of religion, 36, 57, 60, 65, 99
Wycliffe, John, 8, 11–12, 20–22, 29–30, 32, 34

Author Index

Abu Laila, Muhammad, 78n10, 109
Adams, J., 124
Åkerman, Susanna, 41n25, 109
Akkerman, Fokke, 110, 115, 123
Almond, Philip C., 39n16, 109
Anderson, Gary A., 27, 109
Anderson, Paul M., 125
Aquilina, Mike, 22n33, 109
Aquinas, Thomas, 19–20, 30, 98, 101, 109
Armogathe, Jean-Robert, 117, 125
Arnaldez, Roger, 53n88, 78n11, 109
Arnold, Bill T., 105n55, 109
Arnold, Claus, 87n42, 109
Asad, Talal, 53, 94, 95n10, 98n21, 101n34, 109
Ashcraft, Richard, 69n61, 109
Asín Palacios, Miguel, 78n11, 102n42, 109
Augustine, 93, 97, 98n21, 101, 109
Auvray, Paul, 67n53, 110

Barmann, Lawrence, 89n47, 110
Barnouw, Jeffrey, 42n32, 110
Barthélemy, Dominique, 38n10, 44n40, 51n65, 67n52, 110
Bartholomew, Craig G., 113
Baumgold, Deborah, 47n52, 110
Belaval, Yvon, 116
Benbassa, Esther, 123
Benítez, Miguel, 41n23, 110
Bense, W., 124
Berman, Joshua, 4, 110
Bernier, Jean, 40n17–18, 44n40, 48n53, 49n59, 50, 60n20, 67n52, 110
Beyssade, Michelle, 50n61, 110

Bobbio, Norberto, 124
Bourel, Dominique, 116
Bouveresse, Renée, 118
Boyle, John F., 20n24, 110
Brecht, Martin, 26, 110
Bright, Pamela, 101n35, 110
Bucur, Bogdan G., 101n35, 110
Bunce, Robin, 42n29, 110
Burke, Ronald, 118

Callaghan, G. K., 47n50, 110
Calvert, Kenneth R., 4n2, 110
Cameron, Euan, 94n9, 110, 115
Candler, Peter M. Jr., 101n34, 110
Cassuto, Umberto, 4, 110
Cavanaugh, William T., 28, 53, 80n17, 95, 97, 98n20–22, 99–100, 111
Champion, Justin A.I., 82n24, 111
Checchini, Aldo, 124
Christofolini, Paolo, 120
Coleman, Frank M., 81n22, 111
Congar, Yves, 99n26, 111
Cooke, Bernard, 121
Curley, Edwin, 50n60–61, 64n40, 111

Dauphinais, Michael, 110
D'Costa, Gavin, 104n48, 111
de Lubac, Henri, 101n35, 111
den Hollander, A.A., 124
Dixon, C. Scott, 26, 31, 122
Djedi, Youcef, 53n88, 63n35, 111
Dohrmann, Natalie B., 125
Dolansky, Shawna, 114
Domínguez, Atilano, 121
Donagan, Alan, 50n62, 64n40, 111

AUTHOR INDEX

Duffy, Eamon, 22n33, 31n70, 32n72, 80n18, 85n34, 95n13, 111
Dulaey, Martine, 101n35, 111
Dungan, David Laird, 51n65, 52–53, 54n91, 81n23, 111

Elazar, Daniel J., 50n60, 111
Escrivá, Josemaría, 96n17, 111

Farmer, William R., 83n28, 84n32, 94, 105n54, 111, 123
Fasolt, Constantin, x, 88n45, 102n41, 112
Ferraro, Domenico, 120
Fishbane, Michael, 101n37, 112, 114
Foisneau, Luc, 116
Force, James E., 111
Fraenkel, Carlos, 53n88, 63n35, 112
Frampton, Travis L., 26n49, 48n54, 51n65, 53, 63n33, 80n15, 102n41, 102n43, 112
Freedman, R. David, 40n18, 81n23, 112
Freeman, Curtis W., 101n35, 112
Freudenthal, Jakob, 49n59, 53n88, 112
Fubini, Riccardo, 80n14, 112

Gabbey, Alan, 50n62, 64n40, 112
Gabriel, Frédéric, 41n23, 112
Gadenz, Pablo T., 88n43, 112
Gaeta, Giancarlo, 101n35, 112
Galil, Gershon, 116
Gallicet-Calvetti, Carla, 50n60, 112
Garrett, Don, 111–112
Garrido, Juan José, 51n65, 52n86, 112
Gebhardt, Carl, 123
Geerken, John H., 80n14, 112
Gerdmar, Anders, 105n54, 113
Gibert, Pierre, 40n17–18, 50n64, 51n65, 83n25, 94n9, 102n43, 104n50, 106n56, 113
Gigliotti, Gianna, 120
Gillespie, Michael Allen, 42n26, 42n28–29, 43n33, 43n35, 47n50, 53, 98n23, 113
Gisel, Pierre, 123
Gordon, Cyrus H., 4–5, 113
Goris, Harm, 124

Goshen-Gottstein, M.H., 38n10, 80n14, 81n19–20, 92n1, 113
Grafton, Anthony, 38n11, 113
Green, Arthur, 124
Griffiths, Paul J., 94, 95n10, 97n19, 98n21, 113
Gross, Michael B., 83n28, 105n54, 113
Gruntfest, Jacob, 49n58, 113

Haarmann, Ulrich, 39n16, 113
Hahn, Scott W., ix–x, 7–14, 16–22, 23n34, 23n36–37, 24–30, 31n68, 32, 34, 42n26, 42n28–30, 43n33–35, 43n38–39, 44n40–41, 44n43, 45, 46n47–48, 47, 48n54, 49n59, 50n60–61, 51n65, 52n86, 55, 57–61, 62n28–30, 64–74, 79, 87n41, 90n50, 90n52, 94n9, 107, 113
Hallaq, Wael B., 113
Hammill, Graham, 52n86, 66, 114
Haran, Alexander Y., 41n24, 114
Harry, Patricia, 121
Hauerwas, Stanley, 104n48, 114
Hazard, Paul, 67n52, 82n24, 114
Heft, James, 15n13, 114
Hennecke, Susanne, 124
Hermann, Hans-Georg, 117, 119
Hill, Harvey, 86n40, 87n42, 88n44, 114
Hoffmeier, James K., 4, 114
Holloway, Steven W., 105n55, 114
Homan, Michael M., 40n18, 114

Idel, Moshe, 101n37, 114
Israel, Jonathan I., 56, 62, 114, 123

James, Susan, 50n61, 114
Jarick, John, 113, 119
Jodock, Darrell, 114, 116
John Paul II, Pope, 96, 114
Jones, Andrew Willard, x, 12, 15, 17, 26, 29, 100n29, 108, 114
Jorink, Eric, 40n17, 49–50n59, 114

Kaplan, Yosef, 62n33, 115
Kasher, Rimon, 101n37, 115
Katz, David S., 111
Kaufmann, Yehezkel, 4, 115

AUTHOR INDEX

Kelly, J.N.D., 22n33, 115
King, Joshua, 118
Kitchen, K.A., 4, 115
Klepper, Deeana Copeland, 101, 102n40, 115
Klijnsmit, Anthony J., 49n58, 115
Kofsky, Aryeh, 78n9, 115
Krašovec, Jože, 112
Kraus, Hans-Joachim, 94n9, 115
Kugel, James L., 38n10, 44n40, 50n64, 51n65, 77, 78n7, 80n14, 84n30, 100n32, 115
Kuhn, Thomas S., 5n7, 115

La Peyrère, Isaac, 9, 34–42, 44–45, 47–50, 52–55, 63, 67, 81–82, 102n44, 103, 107, 115
Lagrée, Jacqueline, 50n60, 115, 123
Lamberigts, Mathijs, 124
Lapin, Hayim, 120
Laursen, John Christian, 120
Lazarus-Yafeh, Hava, 78n10, 102n42, 115
Lease, Gary, 85n35, 116
Legaspi, Michael C., 83n25–27, 93n3, 100, 102n43, 103–104, 105n55, 106n56, 116
Leijenhorst, Cees, 46n47, 116
Lessay, Franck, 44n40, 116
Levenson, Jon D., 6, 43n33, 54, 84n31, 100, 105–106, 116
Levering, Matthew, ix, 45n33, 46n47, 51n65, 110, 116
Levie, Tirisah, 115
Levy, Ze'ev, 49n58, 116
Lienhard, Joseph T., 112
Little, Donald P., 113
Livingstone, David N., 41n23, 116
Ljamai, Abdelilah, 78n10, 116
Loisy, Alfred, 77, 84, 86–87, 88n44, 89, 116
Lorberbaum, Menachem, 50n60, 116
Löwenbrück, Anna-Ruth, 83n25, 116
Luther, Martin, 8, 12, 20, 25–33, 99, 116

Machinist, Peter, 4n3, 116
Maddox, Graham, 80n14, 116
Mahoney, Edward P., 120

Malcolm, Noel, 40n18, 42n26–29, 42n31, 43n36–37, 44, 45n45–46, 47, 48n53, 49n57, 49n59, 50n60, 116
Malet, André, 52n86, 117
Malherbe, Michel, 81n22, 117
Mandelbrote, Scott, 114
Manrique Charry, Juan Francisco, 50n62, 64n40, 117
Manuel, Frank, 105n54, 117
Marchand, Suzanne, 83n27, 104n48, 117
Marius, Richard, 30n66, 117
Martin, Dale B., 120
Martinich, A.P., 42n26, 42n29, 44n40, 117
Marx, Anthony W., 80n18, 95n13, 117
Marx, Steven, 80n14, 117
Masuzawa, Tomoko, 83n27, 93, 97n19, 117
Mayer, Cornelius P., 101n35, 117
Mazza, Enrico, 45n44, 117
McAuliffe, Jane Dammen, 117, 124–25
McDermott, Ryan, 101n35, 117
McKane, William, 67n52, 117
McKim, Donald K., 123
Melamed, Yitzhak Y., 111, 122
Michman, Jozeph, 115, 125
Miethke, Jürgen, 79n13, 117
Milbank, John, 6, 95, 96n15, 108, 117
Minnis, A.J., 79n12, 101n35, 102n42, 117
Mirri, F. Saverio, 67n53, 118
Misner, Paul, 84n33, 118
Momigliano, Arnaldo, 83n28, 105n54, 118
Moorman, Mary C., 27n53, 118
Moreau, Pierre-François, 50n60, 51n65, 115, 118, 123
Morrow, Jeffrey L., 3, 7n12–13, 9n18, 10n1–3, 11n4–5, 17n17, 31n69, 35n1–2, 36n4–5, 37n6–7, 39n14–15, 40n17–18, 41n23–25, 42n26, 42n28–30, 43n33–35, 43n39, 44n40, 47n51, 48n54, 49n56, 49n59, 50n60, 51n65, 52n86, 55n3, 56n4, 56n5, 58n11, 59n19, 60n20, 62n30, 62n33, 63n34, 63n36, 64n40, 67n52, 77n4–6, 80n16, 81n22–23, 82n24, 83n25,

AUTHOR INDEX

Morrow, Jeffrey L. (*continued*), 86n40, 95n13-14, 96n15, 98n21-22, 99n27, 100n31, 101n34-35, 102n42-44, 103n45, 104n48-49, 107n1, 107n3-6, 118, 122
Mulder, Martin J., 115
Muller, Richard A., 101n38, 119
Müller, Sascha, 67n52, 119

Nadler, Steven, 48n54, 50n60, 51n65, 52n86, 65, 119
Nahkola, Aulikki, 83n25, 119
Nehlsen, Hermann, 79n13, 117, 119
Nellen, H.J.M., 37n7, 49n56, 119
Nelson, Eric, 43n35, 50n60, 53, 98n23, 119
Neto, José R. Maia, 112
Neuhaus, Richard John, 121
Novick, Peter, 88n45, 105n53, 119
Noyes, John K., 105n55, 119

O'Connell, Marvin R., 85, 86n37, 86n40, 119
O'Connell, Matthew J., 117
O'Loughlin, Thomas, 78n7, 119
Osier, Jean Pierre, 50n60, 119

Pacchi, Arrigo, 46n48, 47n51, 50n60, 60, 81n22, 119
Paganini, Gianni, 46n47, 120, 123
Parente, Fausto, 41n24, 81n21, 120
Parkin, Jon, 50n60, 120
Pasto, James, 105n54, 120
Pickstock, Catherine, 98n22, 120
Pietsch, Andreas Nikolaus, 37n7, 41n24-25, 63n36, 120
Pitre, Brant, 88n43, 120
Pius X, Pope, 75, 87, 89, 120
Popkin, Richard H., 37n7, 38, 39n14, 39n16, 40n17, 41n24-25, 47, 48n53-54, 49n56, 49n59, 62-63, 81n21, 120
Portier, William L., x, 6-7, 84n33, 85n34, 85n36, 99n27, 121
Poulat, Émile, 85n36, 121
Preus, J. Samuel, 50, 64, 121
Propp, William Henry, 115

Pulcini, Theodore, 78n10, 121

Quennehen, Élisabeth, 38n12, 41n25, 81n21, 121

Ramón Guerrero, Rafael, 53n88, 63n35, 121
Ratzinger, Joseph, 5-6, 8, 76, 86n38, 89n48, 108n9-10, 121
Rendsburg, Gary A., 4, 121
Reta, José Oroz, 124
Reventlow, Henning Graf, 42n26, 42n28, 44n40, 47n52, 48n54, 82n24, 94n9, 106n56, 111, 121, 123
Rif 'at, Nurshif, 40n18, 122
Rocha, Biff, 95n14, 96n15, 122
Rodrigues, M.A., 49n58, 122
Rogers, G.A.J., 42n29, 116, 122-24
Rogerson, John W., 106n56, 122
Rosenthal, Frank, 79n12, 122
Rosenthal, Michael A., 52n86, 111, 122

Sacksteder, William, 50n60, 122
Sæbø, Magne, 94n9, 119, 122
Schindler, David L., 88n46, 122
Schmidt-Biggemann, Wilhelm, 123
Schochet, Gordon, 116
Schönert, Jörg, 124
Schuhmann, Karl, 42n28, 43n35, 50n60, 122
Schwaiger, Georg, 122
Schweitzer, Albert, 53, 122
Scribner, R.W., 26, 31, 122
Septimus, Bernard, 113
Shadle, Matthew A., 53n89, 122
Sheehan, Jonathan, 83n25, 103, 104n48, 104n50, 105n55, 106, 122
Silberman, Neil Asher, 105n55, 122
Silverthorne, Michael, 123
Simon, Christian, 105n54, 123
Simonetti, Manlio, 101n35, 123
Sinai, Nicolai, 51n65, 123
Skinner, Quentin, 42n28, 123
Sommerville, Johann P., 44-45n43, 123
Sorell, Tom, 46n47-48, 47n49, 116-17, 122-24

AUTHOR INDEX

Spinoza, Baruch, ix, 6–9, 11n4, 13, 25, 34–37, 48–56, 58–59, 62–71, 73–74, 81–82, 84, 102–103, 107, 115, 123
Springborg, Patricia, 46n47–48, 47, 60, 116–17, 120, 123
Stallsworth, Paul T., 8n16, 89n48, 123
Starobinski-Safran, Esther, 39n15, 41n24, 123
Steenbakkers, Piet, 110
Steinmetz, David C., 101n38, 119, 123
Stern, David, 125
Strayer, Joseph R., 100n29, 123
Stroumsa, Guy G., 67n52, 123
Subrahmanyam, Sanjay, 39n16, 124
Synan, Edward, 101n45, 124
Sysling, Harry, 115

Tabet Balady, Miguel Angel, 93n3, 124
Talar, C.J.T., 114
Talmage, Frank, 101n37, 124
Tamer, Georges, 123
Tanner, Norman P., 76n3, 90n51, 96n16, 124
Taylor, Charles, 98n23, 124
Tierney, Brian 15n13, 124
Tilley, Maureen A., 101n35, 124
Titzmann, Michael, 38n10, 124
Torrell, Jean-Pierre, 20n24, 124
Tortarolo, Edoardo, 123
Tricaud, François, 44n40, 124
Troeltsch, Ernst, 14, 124
Troilo, Erminio, 79n12, 124
Tuchman, Barbara, 23n35, 124
Tuck, Richard, 42n28–29, 124
Twersky, Isadore, 113

van Asselt, Willem, 39n15, 124
van Bunge, Wiep, 50n61, 124

van der Coelen, Peter, 101n34, 124
van der Meer, Jitse M., 114
Vardaman, Jerry, 125
Vick, Brian, 83n27, 104n48, 125
Vlessing, Odette, 62, 63n33, 125
Vollhardt, Friedrich, 124

Waldstein, Michael Maria, 102n43, 125
Walfish, Barry D., 101n37, 125
Walker, Adrian, 121
Walther, Manfred, 51n65, 125
Waugh, Evelyn, 97, 125
Weisberg, David B., 105n55, 109
Weiss, David, 122
Wellhausen, J., 2, 4, 36, 38n10, 83, 105, 125
Werner, Winter Jade, 118
Whitman, Jon, 118
Whybray, R.N., 4, 5n6, 125
Wiker, Benjamin, ix–x, 7–14, 16–22, 23n34, 23n36–37, 24–30, 31n68, 32, 34, 42n26, 42n28–30, 43n33–35, 43n38–39, 44n40–41, 44n43, 45, 46n47–48, 47, 48n54, 49n59, 50n60–61, 51n65, 52n86, 55, 57–61, 62n28–30, 64–74, 79, 94n9, 107, 113, 125
Wilken, Robert Louis, 100–101n33–34, 125
Williams, Megan Hale, 93n2, 93n4, 125
Williamson, George S., 104n48, 125
Wineland, John D., 110
Wolfson, Harry Austryn, 53n88, 125
Woodbridge, John D., 82n24, 125

Yamauchi, Edwin M., 4, 78n8, 84n29, 125
Yovel, Yirmiyahu, 50n61, 51n65, 125

Zac, Sylvain, 50n62, 64n40, 126

www.ingramcontent.com/pod-product-compliance
Lightning Source LLC
Chambersburg PA
CBHW071510150426
43191CB00009B/1476